The Wolfhounds

TO: Bob

Trust in God
for all things.

Be Blessed

Rev. J.D. Smith

12/31/05

The Wolfhounds

Reverend Joseph David Smith

VANTAGE PRESS
New York

FIRST EDITION

Copyright © 2002 by Reverend Joseph David Smith

Published by Vantage Press, Inc.
516 West 34th Street, New York, New York 10001

Manufactured in the United States of America
ISBN: 0-533-12987-7

Library of Congress Catalog Card No.: 98-90904

0 9 8 7 6 5 4 3 2

To my beloved wife, Garnetta Carlton; our precious daughters,
Sheriée D'Lon and Brionne Renée; my siblings; and
to all Vietnam Veterans and their families

Contents

Preface   ix

I	My Stay At Bien-Hoa	1
II	What Are You in for Now?	9
III	Are We in Vietnam?	16
IV	Defend Your Life	23
V	Who's the Funny Guy?	30
VI	The RTO	39
VII	The New Lieutenant	47
VIII	The Wolfhounds Claim Victory	61
IX	The Wolfhounds Meet the Regular	
	V.C. Army (NVA)	84
X	The Tet Offensive at Christmas Time	109
XI	Who's Afraid of Walking Point?	129
XII	The Return to the Cambodian Border	143
XIII	How Fast Are You Really?	159
XIV	The Silence of Death, Without	
	Warning a Friend	178
XV	So Long to a Brother, a Friend in Nam	193
XVI	The Trip Home after the Duty	
	on the Mountain	202

Preface

This is a true story, which took place in Vietnam from September 1968 to September 1969.

The recording of this story began in March 1987, at 8:30 P.M. and the writing of this story began November 30, 1992, at 9:00 P.M. The Wolfhounds 1st and 2nd battalion are a part of the 25th Division. I was in Alpha Company of the 2nd battalion of the 25th Division. Each battalion contained approximately 600–800 men.

This book is dedicated to my wife, Garnetta C. Smith, who has stood by me as my friend through my transition period, morally and spiritually; to our two daughters, Sheriée D'Lon Smith and Brionne Renée Smith, who both have been good listeners as I shared age appropriate information regarding my experience; and to my siblings, Robert L. Smith, William H. Smith, Warren Smith, Ida M. Gay, Jannie M. Berry, and Pauline C. Pendergrass, for their moral and spiritual support as I adjust to civilian life upon my arrival home.

For the veterans and other family and friends who are able to read this book, with the understanding and empathy for the pain, I and perhaps many other Vietnam brothers have carried from Vietnam until now: pray for me and all the veterans to have a healthy life.

I am the fifth child of eight children in my family and was nineteen years old when I was drafted into the United States Army. Upon receiving my orders to go to Vietnam, I did not know what to expect. One of my many thoughts was *Why me?, and not one of my older male siblings.*

I intended for twelve years to write this book, but was emotionally unable to start, because of the pain I endured from my tour of duty in Vietnam. However, I give thanks to God Almighty for the strength and courage to persevere until the completion of my book. I present to you *The Wolfhounds*.

The Wolfhounds

I

My Stay at Bien-Hoa

I arrived in Vietnam on September 18, 1968, at the Bien-Hoa Airport. From there, we were transported to a holding area approximately three miles from the Bien-Hoa Airport. During this trip to our holding area our bus backfired; the sound was like a fifty-caliber machine gun being used to shoot at the bus. Because of this sound everyone jumped out of their seats and dived for the floor of the bus. I was on the bottom first.

Everyone was frightened from the backfiring sound of the bus. The bus driver told us that it was okay, the noise was the bus. We all returned to our seats feeling a little embarrassed, but managed to remain in our seats and arrived at the holding area without any further incidents.

While in the holding area, we all waited to have our names called for assigned battalion. However, until our names were called for our battalion listed on the roster, everyone was assigned to kitchen patrol (KP).

Later that day there was roll call. Some of the guys left for their battalion and did not do KP. Another roll call at 6:00 P.M.: 30 guys left for battalion assignments. Unfortunately, my name was not included. Therefore, I was assigned to KP, which started at 4:00 A.M.

As I laid on the bunk before the last roll call, I recalled the view on the street that the bus traveled through. The tall grass, the small hooches, and the people cooking their food squatted down near an open low fire as the entire view

1

gave the street a slum look.

Everyone wore bamboo hats because they were farmers. They grew rice in the fields behind their hooches. These hats were very large. They were so large that if you squatted down in the rice field you would look like a dry rice stalk, body and face not visible, that's what Sir Charles did, with his hat. I later got up and headed for the mess hall.

After eating at the mess hall that night around 7:00 P.M. I left to return to my assigned barracks not far from the mess hall. As I entered the barracks I noticed holes in the building caused by scrapped metal from the Viet Cong RPG (Rocket Propelled Grenade) rockets and mortar rounds.

At this time a guy not only told me of the RPG rockets and mortar rounds, but that the Viet Cong (Sir Charles) had also entered the base Bien-Hoa grounds. Just then a chill went through my body as I wondered how I would defend myself knowing that I had no weapon.

I stepped on the bottom bunk, lifting myself to the top bunk that I had selected, which was on the first floor in this barracks. As I laid back down before roll call that night, I prayed that God would be with me and the others as we tried to rest this night. There was light weapon fire that night at a distance.

Roll call was announced at 9:00 P.M. for personnel to leave in the morning to join their battalion. Again my name was not called so I went back to the barracks and laid on my bunk, thinking about being in this place away from my family, realizing that they did not have a clue as to what I was truly involved in, being here, in Vietnam.

Had I not gone into the service, it would have caused problems for my parents. But there were many times I considered escaping to Canada, before I went to New Haven's induction center.

I didn't know what God's plans were for me, so I only viewed what was obvious and my thoughts were how slim my chances appeared, in Vietnam, on going home.

While in Fort Dix, in New Jersey, I was told that I had been selected for Vietnam. I qualified because of my expert shooting at target range, with my M–16. Shooting at targets is one thing because targets never shoot back and they are always in the same place, in front and not crawling on the ground, or in a tree, or in a hole in the ground.

No, this was not the wild west movies that I enjoyed watching on television or Rody Yates on Rawhide. This was not a World War I or II movie; this was advanced action and the real movies were not available yet. Yes, my brothers and sisters were home watching television, while I was here bleeding inside, nervous, in a cold sweat, many tears in my heart and eyes.

I missed my family and I wanted to go home, but I couldn't because if I walked off the post I could be captured by Sir Charles and maybe killed, so I finally went off to sleep.

I guess morning arrived, and I had to pull KP. This was much earlier than I realized. There was someone moving in the barracks going from bunk to bunk. I thought he was Sir Charles, killing as he moved down the aisle in my direction. I had nothing but my hands, and I was going to do my best to get him before he got me. I didn't get up to run because I thought he may have had a gun, and that my chances would be better if I played as if I was still asleep.

And then he came near my bunk and said, "It's time to get up, you're on KP." I jumped, but was truly relieved that it was someone from the mess hall. I then got up and went to the bathroom to wash up and then went on my way to the mess hall. I was assigned to washing pots and pans in the kitchen.

One guy had been in Vietnam for two years, because of the combat or hazardous duty pay. He said he is making more money in Vietnam than if he remained in the United States and he was thinking of doing one more year. It was time for breakfast at 6:00 A.M. After breakfast I could see and feel the time passing on: 6:00, 7:00, 8:00, 9:00 A.M.

I turned my thinking back to the pots and pans. I noticed about a hundred and fifty yards away a person squatting down. It looked like a wall; it was in black pajamas. I didn't know what to do. So I kept a watchful eye on this person in the black pajamas and then I went in and told this guy that I saw someone squatting. He said, Oh, that's mama-san, she is using the outside toilet.

This had been the third incident that I had encountered that caused an increase in my blood pressure; the ride on the bus, the guy from the mess hall, and now mama-san in black pajamas with a bamboo hat on her head.

When we were in Fort Pork, which is located in Louisiana, our Army trainers told us different signs we needed to be aware of; an object that appeared to be out of place from its surroundings, and things that look like they should be part of the location, but are not.

At the 6:00 P.M. roll call I was told that I would be going to my assigned battalion on September 20, 1968, so I went to the barracks to prepare my bags for the next day's trip.

But I had mixed thoughts about going to my new battalion. I wanted to remain on KP, because I did not want to go to the 25th Division where I would be assigned and sent out into the jungles to fight. But if I remained in the holding area in Bien-Hoa I would not have a weapon and this holding area had been over-run by the Viet Cong before. Tough decision.

After I got off KP about 9:00 P.M. that night there were some military police (MPs) running around to find a Viet

Cong lady. She had cut one of the soldiers who went into town to have a good time. The soldier left with this girl, unaware that she was a Viet Cong and that she had a razor blade inserted in her vagina. Upon sexual intercourse, the soldier was cut.

This was the reason the MPs were looking for this young lady and any other Viet Cong that may have been with her. They caught her and rushed the soldier to the hospital. I said, Oh man, these were some of things I had heard while growing up that took place during World War II in Japan. I shook my head and went to the barracks thinking that it is real dangerous over here; you can't even trust the women.

So I showered and went to my bunk. I had worked from 4:00 A.M. until 9:00 P.M. that night in the mess hall.

The Viet Cong decided to send RPG rockets into the complex. I could hear the people screaming and yelling Incoming rounds run for the bunkers. Scrapped metal from the rounds ran through the building outer wall as though it was paper. I was so tired that I just laid there and prayed as I looked out through the screens on the windows and saw the flames from the rounds that had just exploded. Then I realized that this was truly a war and there was nowhere to go.

But I knew that my faith in God would protect me, because I was only nineteen years old and wanted to be married and have children someday. Finally I went off to sleep, and awoke the next morning, September 20, 1968. At the mess hall that morning some of the guys asked, How was your night sleep?

I told them that it was fine and that I did get some rest even with the incoming rounds. After breakfast everyone returned to their barracks and waited for the 9:00 A.M. roll call. At this time, myself and six other guys' names were called, assigning us to the 25th Division.

The next day September 21, 1968, I returned to Bien-Hoa Airport to board a B-52 bomber airplane, which would transport me and the other guys to our battalion.

I didn't know anyone in this holding area, but made it my place to talk to these Caucasians and African-American guys while I was there with them. The guys in the mess hall were glad and sad that I had been assigned to a battalion.

That's the way it was with most Americans (Caucasian and African-Americans) in Vietnam. There was a sense of understanding that never surfaced before, I guess because this was the first real war where Caucasians and African-Americans spent a great deal of their time together, more than they had in World War I and II.

This war, Vietnam, was also different in many ways than all the other wars. There has always been a front line, where firing of rounds was exchanged from trenches, or you can call it a stand-off position of battle. But, the Vietnam war had no known front line. If there was one it was in front of you, or was it on the side of you, or was it behind you? Wherever you camped for that night, out there was your front line.

As I was leaving, the guys in the mess hall kitchen they gave me a hug and you know the Brothers (African-Americans) gave up that bad handshake with the power sign.

At this point I was strengthened by the closeness from all the guys I had just met two days ago and did not want to leave them. There was more truth from Caucasians' lips at that time than any other time I had heard in the past. Everyone removed the tears from their eyes with a bit of anger that they may never see me again. I understood this feeling, which drew me closer to God for my protection.

I ran to the bus and took a seat. As I looked out of the window as the bus pulled off, I saw the faces of those guys standing, awaiting their assigned battalion. The guys in the mess hall kitchen saw many guys coming and going in and out of Vietnam. Many of the faces the guys in the mess hall kitchen never saw again. Yes, it was sad. Then I looked at the guys awaiting to be assigned to their battalion, their faces sad. Most faces were still in shock just being in Vietnam, like me.

I had always enjoyed watching war movies on television, but never wanted to really be in or to be part of any war, but there I was truly going off to battle. Now I was assigned to a battalion.

The bus would return us to the Bien-Hoa Airport for flight to our assigned battalion. Just then I thought of a World War II movie: when the plane was going to land it was shot down and everyone had to parachute from the plane.

The bus was escorted from the holding area to Bien-Hoa by two armed jeeps driven by the military police (MPs). One jeep was in front of the bus and the other follow behind the bus, with machine guns mounted, in case we became under attack from the Viet Cong (The North Vietnamese).

The bus travelled back through the same village area that we had passed on our way to the holding area two days ago. The people in the village were squatting cooking their meals over the open fire as I and the rest rode by on the bus wondering what could we do if we were under attack.

So I prayed because of my uncomfortable position of not being able to defend myself. Thank God, that we arrived safely at the Bien-Hoa Airport grounds. As we stood up to walk off the bus there was a feeling of relief that we did not experience any attack back to the Bien-Hoa Airport.

Our wait was about ten to fifteen minutes before we

were able to board the B-52 bomber plane. The plane was painted with colors of light green, dark green, brown, and beige for camouflage. This allowed the plane to go undetected when on the ground or flying close to the tops of the trees, blending in with the terrain so that it would not be easily spotted by the enemy.

The seven of us boarded the B-52 bomber plane. Inside, there were not any of the comfortable seats or acoustic wall panels to reduce the sound of the engine as is done with the commercial airplanes.

Yes, the color of the plane, the noise in the plane, required you to yell. Even if the person was looking at you, he would have to read your lips, he still would not be able to hear you. This plane was very noisy to me. We had to use hand signals in order to ensure that you were able to understand the officer's direction to enforce the care we needed for each other while riding on the plane.

We finally arrived at this one-man airport in the 25th Division battalion airfield. We departed from the rear of the B-52 plane and boarded the army truck that awaited our arrival. A few of the seven were assigned to the MPs, and some were assigned to Alpha, Bravo, Charlie, and Delta company within the 25th Division.

I was assigned to Alpha company along with another guy named Edward Dow. This other guy named Charles Madlock was assigned to Charlie company.

II

What Are You in for Now?

We had to attend an orientation section for two or three weeks before we actually went into the field (jungle). Everyone assigned to the 2nd Battalion of the 25th Division, all new arrivals for Alpha, Bravo, Charlie, and Delta companies, were expected to attend the training session.

That afternoon there was a briefing on how we should conduct ourselves while in Vietnam and that caution was to be used if we wanted to play around with these Vietnamese women.

The sergeant told us that you can catch venereal diseases, of the worse kind, black balls, where they could never allow you to return to the United States for fear of you spreading these dangerous diseases that would kill people.

He told us about the Viet Cong women inserting razor blades in their vaginas to kill American soldiers, and how some of the women arrived each morning to work on the base, where they might plant bombs or place ground up glass in food or chipped-up nails or other items that could be placed in something we had to eat or drink.

As the sergeant continued talking I reflected back on the type of training I had received in Fort Pork, in Louisiana.

Most of the sergeants at Fort Pork had completed one or two tours of duty in Vietnam and was confronted with many combat gun fights. I felt the sergeants at Fort Pork pushed us very hard to increase our chances of making it home alive by teaching how to read maps, compasses, and making it with or without water or food for a day or so.

This is how it was done at Fort Pork as part of our training. We would also rise very early each morning for exercise around 4:00 A.M. The reason for this early-morning exercise was that Louisiana was very hot and humid, a climate much like that of Vietnam. They had constructed a place like that in Vietnam, with a village, a water buffalo pit filled with water to smell like water buffalo, and rice fields filled with water.

We had to walk through the rice fields and the water buffalo pit which left our clothes we wore smelling as bad as the toilet. We had to read our compass and look at our maps to find the location the sergeants had for us, to find our food, at the top of a hill.

But if we did not make it to the top of the hill by noon that day you had no food or water until the next day. Yes, we played jungle warfare in Louisiana, and many things that had taken place here had to be applied in the real environment now.

One day some of the sergeants and a few of the other soldiers were to be the Viet Congs. They gave us blank adapters to place on our weapons for shooting when we were under attack. As we walked through the village area I quietly passed the word to be careful entering the village.

I was point man with another guy and four others walked flank as we approached the village. There was much smoke in the air, which this made it very difficult to see and we needed to be very careful of the booby traps. I noticed that there was movement. I had spotted this earlier; it was on the outside of the village area and not in the center, so I approached the hooch from the left side.

Just then a guy from the right flank walked into the

center of the village, setting off the first booby trap. After hearing the explosion, everyone dropped to the ground. Gunfire rang out. We then returned gunfire to hooch, where we thought the gunfire was coming from. They ran from the hooch and then the gun firing stopped.

We slowly raised up from the ground, moving breathlessly through the village, checking for the enemy. One guy entered a hooch and gunfire rang out again. We did not return gunfire in the direction of that hooch, because we thought that we might hit our own man. Then we all moved in slowly on that hooch and the Viet Cong appeared around back. We opened fire again on the VC enough to stop him.

We then checked the remaining hooches, noticing that everyone was booby trapped. As we backed off from each of the hooches, one guy noticed that there was a pile of rocks in the center of the village that was also booby trapped.

We backed off from the entire village, moving to a safe area to discuss our next assignment. While in the safety area, we decided to eat our C-ration as the sergeant told us about the things we had done wrong in this exercise.

The sergeant told us that we were too close together as we entered the village and that Sir Charles could have killed all of us if this was a real combat situation. He also said we waited too long for the Viet Cong to come out of the hooch. We should have assaulted or attacked the hooch because the soldier that went in the hooch in a real-life situation would have come out immediately.

So, we should have assumed him dead and attacked the hooch. Also, that time lag would have allowed Sir Charles to trigger the booby trap in the center of village, killing even more GIs.

The sergeant stated that timing with caution was

always needed. We then got our gear and loaded up on the army truck going to another location. As we proceeded down the road, out of the blue an explosion went off. Everyone jumped out of the truck and got behind or on the side of it and started returning gunfire in the wooded area.

The sergeants then said, Assault the wooded area. The guys started moving out in front, firing their weapons as they moved forward. They could not see anyone as they moved to the end of their assault line. Just then Sir Charles (the other soldiers) popped up out of the ground and started firing their weapons at the backs of the assault team.

I saw what was going on and then I started running in the direction of the assault team, shooting Sir Charles the Viet Congs in their backs in order to save some of our soldiers.

The sergeant told me after the assault drill that I should have been with the assault team and had not remained behind the truck.

I told the sergeant if we did this in Vietnam we would all be sent home in a body bag and if they are looking for me to do this in Vietnam, without looking for cover first, they are crazy.

My father and mother did not raise a fool, and I thought you said we need to think when we are in the jungle. These guys didn't think. I would have been the only one still alive in a real combat situation. After we finished, we got back on the truck to return to our camp location to prepare for our night combat training.

Well, these exercises along with the terrain made us feel like we were already in Vietnam. We had to camp out for three weeks, which meant sleeping on the ground. There were plenty of snakes at Fort Pork, in Louisiana. There were black, corral, rattlers, and water snakes, and wild boars.

Where we set up our camp, water was not available for either washing, or drinking. Because of the rainy weather and the hot temperatures in Louisiana we use the rain to wash up at times. Well, wouldn't you know, the air was filled with many different types of odors.

During the three weeks we reviewed, map reading, compass reading, hand-to-hand combat, morse code, guard patrol procedures, and the operations of the radio (pick-25). We went into the tear gas chambers, tested for jungle warfare, and, to put all we had learned together, for a practice we had a night survival mission. This night survival mission was difficult; the main objective was not to be captured by the other team, the Viet Cong who would interrogate you when you were caught.

This exercise took place about 10:00 P.M.. That night there were two missions: (1) to locate a stake deep in the wooded area. It was really dark out that night, and the moon was our only light as we tried to locate the stake by using our compass. This was a challenge to us. In using our compass, we read it by the moon light to cross many areas, traveling about five miles in the night; (2) to arrive at a safety zone without being captured.

I had met this guy named Hudson. He was in my platoon but that night his compass readings were different then mine. That evening for supper we had to cook or boil our meal, a chicken or steak, and eat it if we wanted to eat that evening. The guys with me did not know what to do with the chicken, so I cleaned it and washed it off, then placed it in a can to boil it.

I let it boil until it was done then we all took a piece. Some of the inner parts were still uncooked, but we had to move on to prepare for our night mission. There were many guys in the woods pretending to be the Viet Cong and we did not want to be caught. It was 10:00 P.M. We moved very slowly through the wooded area, trying not to get caught.

After everyone was in the wooded area, about fifty to a hundred yards in, I began hearing guys screaming that they had been captured. Just then two guys started running in my direction. I squatted down very slowly. They stopped and said, Where did he go? and then they ran off further into the woods. I didn't notice when I had squatted down that there was someone about one hundred feet from me, moving very slowly in my direction.

But he had lost his direction, where I was hiding, so he ran off before I left that spot. Looking around, I saw an open area where the moon shone brighter than any other area on all movement across the open field.

I slowly moved to the opening and walked across the field out of the wooded location. Two Caucasian guys ran out of the woods, so I ran off. They said, Wait, we are not on the other team. Just then Hudson, a brother, popped up from his hiding place.

So the four of us went together and had to cross the water stream, but the area did not look that great to Hudson and me so we said, Let's go down some more, because once you cross the water stream you're back into the woods. The two Caucasian guys crossed the water stream and the Viet Cong team caught them. We heard the screaming and then saw four or five other guys run after us so we went into another spot in the woods to hide.

Hudson and I stayed there until these guys had left the area. Then fifteen minutes later Hudson and I pulled out our compass to find our direction for the targeted area of arrival. We were heading northeast. We had two more miles to travel. It must have been 2:00 A.M. when we finally arrived near the compound of the Viet Cong team, where they were waiting for the rest of us to arrive.

They didn't hear us or see us but we heard them talking so we went around another way and watched them carefully, so that we would be able to make it to the free zone. The sergeant then called his team, the Viet Cong, to come in. We waited until they had moved from their hiding place, then we ran to the free zone. Five of the Viet Cong guys ran after us, but Hudson and I were too quick; we made it in time.

The three sergeants then said we had to end this exercise because the time was very late and there were guys not accounted for at this time.

The three guys finally arrived about 3:30 A.M. Then we were able to return to our camp site. We performed night patrol and used the star-light-scope to identify movement at night. The sergeant in Vietnam asked me was I listening to what he was saying. I said yes sir, I was. I heard him even though my thoughts were in Fort Pork, Louisiana.

The sergeant told us of these venereal diseases and if anyone caught black balls they would be placed on an island with other people from Vietnam that had this venereal disease forever. The sergeant said, If you plan to be sexually active you better go to the PX (Purchase Exchange) and purchase some protection or write home so your relatives can send condoms to you.

He said, Please do not buy any condoms from any Vietnamese person because they could have put small pin holes in the condoms, which would allow you to catch this venereal disease. Some of the guys already had condoms on them that they purchased at home, so they were cool for now. The sergeant told us that we would go through a ten-day training course before going to the field.

This would help adjust our bodies to the climate and reinforce our thinking on survival in the field.

III

Are We in Vietnam?

The training session did place your mind into the environment of Vietnam and affirmed that this was a war and not a game. During the training class we saw many different pictures of Sir Charles (The Viet Cong).

We were paired off to participate in hand-to-hand combat, weapon assault-line, finding mines and disarming them without exploding, identifying booby traps, setting up claymore mines, how to walk on a rice paddy dice, and how caution should be used if you see these items: tires, cigarette lighters, shoes, etc. hanging in the trees or just on the ground. They could be booby trapped.

The sergeants provided training for this class session for more than twenty guys all from the 2nd battalion of the 25th Division. More of the training was on the assault and other maneuvers that would allow us to have the advantage over Sir Charles, when he was in a trench or holes in the ground.

The psychological affects of this training forced us into the awareness of our purpose for being in Vietnam. This training would be for three weeks unless an emergency occurred in the field, causing the training session to be cut short and us to be sent out to the field to carry out the regular patrol duties.

As our unit had done before, they were under attack and lost several men in a battle with the Viet Cong army. But this did not happen so the next day the sergeant told us about a hedged roll (a thick tree line or brushes). Each morning we had to report to the training session by 8:00 A.M. after breakfast in the mess hall.

This wasn't too bad because we were able to shower and put on clean clothes once or twice a day. The training lasted from 8:00 A.M. until 9:00 P.M. each day, but it was far better than being in the fields. Sometimes you felt like you were not in a military war.

In Vietnam the moon normally appeared on the three last days of the month and remained visible for the next five days of the subsequent month. Otherwise, it was moonless and always dark out except for the lights from some buildings and a few light poles in the officers' and some sergeants' quarter areas. There has always been a large number of Vietnamese women that remained in the CU-Chi area after the gates where closed. By that time it would be night and was dark.

Some of these women were hooch girls (they clean the officers' and the sergeant hoochs and sometime granted them some pleasures or a good time). Every man that attended the training session received an assigned weapon, without live ammunition (ammo) because they would issue us blanks to use in the training area, which we transported with us daily. The next day, September 24, 1968, Charles Madlock and I were walking back to the barracks, but because of the darkness Madlock and I came up with a strategy if we came under attack from any Viet Cong that may have entered the base during the course of that day.

Madlock took the right flank and I took the left flank, as we proceeded slowly down this dark road to the barracks. We had to be careful; after a few days of training, we understood that anything could happen. There was a light on in this area and we saw this person moving like they had killed or hit someone over the head.

Madlock and I proceeded very slowly in that direction of this person, a Viet Cong, to overtake him or her as we recalled, to ourselves, that we did not have any ammo.

Therefore, we stated that we would use our weapons as a club. We walked over to the door of the building and the women cried out, NO! Viet Cong!, NO! Viet Cong! NO! Viet Cong! She was trying to tell us not to shoot, because she was a Vietnamese. It threw us off guard, but we felt that we had the enemy.

An MP (Military Policeman) was driving by. He stopped and came over to where we were, Madlock said, someone better speak up we are out here and we don't know what's going on.

The MP had seen the lady and told us that this lady is okay, she's Vietnamese. We left and went on our way to the barracks. That was another added pressure that we had to deal with; not ever knowing who was in our base parameter after it becomes night and it's dark here.

Edward Dow had left earlier that day, before it became dark, because he had to see the headquarters company commander. He was escorted back in a jeep to the barracks.

As time went on for the remaining training session, Madlock was not able to complete his training because of heavy casualties in his company, Charlie Company.

That night Ed, Madlock, and I went around Cu-Chi and stopped and at some of the clubs in other areas to party with Madlock before his departure the next morning. Madlock did not drink a lot, because of his focus on the next day. We did more talking and wiping the tear drops away from our eyes that night. Madlock's company was camped further down in the southern part of Vietnam. The next morning Madlock was ready to take the convoy to his company location.

After 12 days of training Madlock left, but Ed and I

hugged Madlock and then gave up the brother's hand shake. We told Madlock to be cool and don't be a hero in the field. We had tears in our eyes for him, and prayed for his safety.

Ed and I said that Madlock would make it just like we can make it if we stay down and find out where the gunfire is coming from. So we walked to the training center that day without Madlock, wishing that he could still be here, knowing that our time was just around the corner, a few weeks from now.

Later that day we had lunch just as we did every day; just not with Madlock today. The training went well and it was dark again as it is at the end of every training day. Ed and I walked back to the barracks wondering what Madlock was doing this night. We made it back to the barracks and there was this Caucasian guy talking about the field (jungle).

I will not forget this Caucasian guy who would come into our barracks and tell us of the horror that had taken place in the fields. He said that he just left the field and was still recovering from the wounds in the last fire fight. We had been in-country now for almost three weeks and to hear these stories led Ed and me to come up with a plot in order to stay in Cu-Chi for as long as we could.

Ed and I never knew what the action in the field (jungle) was really like. This guy telling us all that happened did frighten us. This guy with blond hair, an Ivy-league type of fellow with a big mouth, talked all the time.

As our three weeks came and left, we had a better understanding of guerrilla warfare, but I was in no rush to test how good it was any time soon. Ed and I spent about two weeks longer in Cu-Chi than we should have, according to what the other guys did after their training.

It really was not the fault of Ed's and mine, because all

the other eighteen guys' names were called each morning so they would join up with their assigned companies. They just never called Ed's or my name during the first five days after training, and then the roll-calling just stopped.

Well, do you think that Ed and I were going to volunteer to go out to the field to hurry up and get shot? No way, Brother. So each morning, noon and at suppertime, we had hot meals and were able to still have showers two or three times a day and change our clothes daily if we needed, too.

We had spit-shine boots and pressed fatigues, and went to the enlisted men's health club for our bath, where the Vietnamese ladies would give us a massage that really relaxed you all over. Ed and I had also been to the officers' health club about twice. The ladies looked better there.

We had seen a few sister officers and some that were enlisted, but when they saw our rank on our collars they turned their heads and walked away. The sisters that were in Nam gave it up to the Caucasian officers and any brother that was an officer or one that pretended to be one. The Caucasian women only dated the African-American or Caucasian men in the basic camp (Cu-Chi). Jungle fighting men were left out.

Anyway, even though we wanted to hang with the sisters, but were unable to, we still had a good time in the rear and not out there wherever that was, with our company (Alpha) fighting Sir Charles.

Things were going smoothly because we were up each morning and only returned to the area for lunch. Otherwise Ed and I would go to the PX, and walk around Cu-Chi (the base camp), which was like a small town about five miles in diameter.

In this base camp beside the 25th Division there were 1st Calvary, the 41st Infantry, 5th Armor Unit and, you guessed it, the 101 Airborne Rangers. By the way, you know the Caucasian blond-haired guy that told us about the contact in the field? Well, he also told us that the Viet Cong had a thousand dollar bounty for every Wolfhound scalp.

We asked around and others said that it was true, so you see all of these things helped Ed and me to remain in the rear as long as we could. One day Ed and I saw one of the convoy trucks with dead soldiers in black bags, which did not sit well with us. That's why we stayed in Cu-Chi.

Anyhow, this other unit always got ambushed when they were leaving the parameter of Cu-Chi and would need to call the Wolfhounds to get the Viet Cong off their backs.

During this time Ed and I were able to become partners, good friends. You see, Ed was from Houston, Texas and was dating, with thoughts of marriage once he returned home from the service. And me, well, I am from Hartford, Connecticut, and had dated different young ladies, but no one special.

I told Ed of my family and he told me about his. It was fun getting to know so much about someone you just met for a few weeks and thinking, I never really knew that guy in the neighborhood that well. Well, as you could imagine, good times, the party times were near their end, and we were unaware of it truly happening to us.

Hey, everyone had seen Ed and me in the company area for days. We even spent time talking to the sergeant, captains, and other enlisted men that came in from the field every now and then. So you see, people knew who we were and where we were, right?

Wrong. We had written letters to our families and friends and had not received any mail in three weeks. If Ed and I were aware that it takes three to four weeks before the mail arrived to the United States we would not have made this mistake.

We walked over to the orderly room and asked the

clerk that morning, was there any mail for Smith and Dow. The guy in the orderly room turned around and said Smith and Dow as he began searching through the mail, but could not find any. Then he said, Smith and Dow are you guys suppose to be in the field? We said, no, our names were never called.

Just then a Lieutenant came in the orderly room. As the corporal started talking to the Lieutenant, Ed and I walked out of the orderly room, moving quickly to the barracks. We did not want to go out to the field. Yes, we were afraid.

Just then, as we were fifty feet away from the barracks, the Lieutenant that was in the orderly room called out, Smith and Dow, front and center. Now! We turned and ran back in the direction of the Lieutenant.

He said, The corporal tells me that you guys are to be sent to the field. He continued, There's a convoy leaving this afternoon about 1:00 P.M.

We said that we did not have any ammo or weapon because the weapons we were assigned for training had to be returned on the last day of class. So the lieutenant and the corporal found two M–16s and some ammo magazines that looked like someone purposely poured dirt down the gun barrel and into the trigger housing. Ha ha, the magazines were in the same condition. All that Ed and I could see by looking at the M–16s and those magazines was a body bag.

IV

Defend Your Life

Ed and I looked around our company area, viewing every building, vehicle, tree, and street. Then we finally focused our eyes upon a fifty gallon drum that had been cut in half to be used for the purpose of cleaning weapons and magazines.

The corporal gave us some LSA lubricant oil for our weapons and magazines to apply once they were clean. Sand was poured down the barrow of the M–16s as well as on the magazines. It rained six or seven times a day, so we felt that the cleaning solution might no longer hold the strength to clean the weapons and magazines, because it had been diluted from the rains.

We were getting ready for combat. Everything prior to this was not for real. All that Ed and I learned since we had been in the army had to now work like a hand-crafted clock. My blood pressure, I knew, must have been a thousand, but that would not get me out of going to the field. The medic just would have said, It's normal.

As we began to clean these dirty weapons, tears began flowing from one eye. As the pain finally reached the other eye, that eye then started to flow. Our tears dropped into the cleaning solution, but we continued to clean the weapons and the magazines. Ed started cursing with anger. Then he almost gave up and said let us just put these guns together and go. I said, No man, don't do this. Ed began cleaning his weapon again.

For one moment Ed and I removed the tears from our eyes, and we looked at each other as if this was going to be the last time for us having a good time, as friends. We felt the good times had just ended for good.

The tears began again, but this time as they flowed, our noses began to run as well. It was painful, imagining what might possibly happen to us on this convoy that would take us to the location of our company.

After thirty minutes of cleaning and crying, Ed and I gave up the brother's hand shake. Then we wiped our eyes and noses, and loaded the forty magazines with ammunition. Placing our web belt and claymore bag with our ammunition, on our shoulders, and the backpacks with some socks, underwear, grenades, we walked to the truck that was part of the convoy.

We cleaned the weapons and the magazines so well that the rounds in the magazines, as we tested them, popped up very smoothly. They had not been field stripped like this in some time, I bet.

The LSA oil was poured into the weapon trigger housing and the magazine's for smooth working. The oil was also used as a coolant when the weapon was fired repeatedly. We had twenty magazines, a piece, plus the one magazine inserted in the M–16. Ready for whatever might come our way. Nervous, yes, but ready. No more tears.

But we wanted to hear from our families and friends, to receive some mail. Well, was it smart on our part? Good question.

We got on the truck and noticed that there were sand bags on the sides and floor of the truck. Man I could have dropped. A cold sweat developed. Ed and I tried to hold back the tears, but man we knew this army convoy was something only seen on television.

Ed and I worked on our strategy to protect each other

and the convoy. Would you believe, on top of everything, we had fears of being in the last truck. Oh Lord!

Having the ability to move from side-to-side to take care of any action that may return fire to the rear, it was covered. We went so far as to tell each other that if one of us gets wounded, to yell out, so the other person would be able to cover the side you received the heavy gun firing from.

The sides of the truck were about two feet high. The driver of our truck was a Caucasian guy. You know I don't know what color the other drivers in the convoy were. I guess my focus wasn't on that right now. Man this is dangerous. I even asked God in a silence, Pray to forgive me and asked Him what I have done to deserve this type of punishment.

Let me tell you something. I have always been in the church, unlike Ed, who smoked, drank, cursed, and played around with many women. Every now and then he went to the church. Man this was unfair. Maybe I should have done all those things Ed did, and then I would not have felt traded by God.

My heart was overflowing in tears, but it wasn't evident on my face, for it had the look of someone angry and afraid. Ed and I looked at each other, but there was not a smile present from either of us. We were in a combat zone now.

Then the lieutenant came out of the orderly room and said, Is everyone ready? Oh, where are Smith and Dow? Right here Sir, we said. Then the convoy pulled off. As we rode through the streets of Cu-Chi our base camp, we thought that this was going to be the last time.

Ed finally said, Well Joe, we had an opportunity to enjoy some of the things in Cu-Chi more than any of the other guys in our training class. I said, Yes, you're right Ed.

Then my voice cracked, but I wanted to say more.

We were told that our company (Alpha) was set up under the Phu-Vinh bridge and it was about a five mile drive from Cu-Chi. As the convoy left the secure parameter of Cu-Chi, we locked-and-loaded our weapons. Now we were ready. We were on the road to the Phu-Vinh bridge.

Alpha sustained heavy losses in combat, so it was set up for our company to guard the bridge so they could receive new troops added to the company before engaging in heavy Viet Cong action. This took place around the 12th of October, 1968.

As the convoy moved slowly down the road, traveling about twenty miles per hour, Ed and I looked at everything in the fields for a Viet Cong person. It would have been unfair if the truck blew up and we did not have a chance to use our weapons that we had prepared just for this battle.

We kept moving from side-to-side, side-to-rear, rear-to-front, so that Sir Charles would not have an easy target to hit. We watched the tall elephant grass. We thought it was Sir Charles moving through the tall grass but it was just the wind blowing the tall grass on this windy day.

We thought that we saw one of the Vietnamese people reach into the rice basket for a weapon, but they just were emptying the smaller basket of rice into a larger one.

This little girl and boy were running up to the truck. Ed and I thought they had a mine attached to their bodies to blow us away. Man, you know this was a trip for us, blood pressure still 400, heart beat 2000, sweat none, tears one or two, ready on the trigger, ready on the trigger. Then we told the children to move back from the truck, so that they would not get hurt. Oh, man, what a relief, the children did not have anything. They just wanted some GI C-ration, but we had none.

Finally as the convoy turned the corner we stopped.

Ed and I both said, What happened? They said, Oh, nothing, they're just checking this part of the road for booby trappers. We said, What! Then the driver said, Do you guys want to stay on the truck or walk on the side of the truck like the demo guy? They are mine sweeping the road. We wanted to say yes, but we wanted to say no, because we did not want to step wrongly, you know what I mean.

Then the driver said, If you guys are getting off the truck, walk in the same steps as the demo guy. Stay about thirty feet behind him, because two other guys stepped on a mine last week; they went home in a body bag.

Neither Ed nor I knew if this guy was telling us the truth. Well, we stayed on the truck. I was too nervous and Ed said he was, too, to be walking. This mine sweep was the length of a football field at this part in the road. It took forever to get inside the Alpha company's parameter.

But, safety first. It seemed like a two-hour road sweep. It may not have been that long, but it was long and frightening. We made it in the parameter. Ed and I were escorted to the CO (Commanding Officer) headquarters. I had a terrible headache and my legs were weak. On our way down we looked on both sides of the road. There were bunkers and guys were standing on the bunkers cheering us on.

They said, Hey we have some newbys, guys added to our squad, hey! Welcome to the Wolfhounds, guys. We smiled and continued walking in the direction where the captain quarters were located.

The captain quarters were under the bridge, along with the first Sergeant, the cooks, and the command post (CP). Once Ed and I arrived at the CP, the first Sergeant greeted us and then welcomed us to Alpha company.

The sergeant also told us to stay out of trouble. Keep your noses clean, and if we see or know of anyone that's on dope, to let him know. He said he's aware that there is dope smoking taking place and did not want us to become part of the group that was doing it.

The sergeant said you must be ready for action whenever the Viet Cong attack, but if you are smoking dope, your timing will be very slow and others can get killed along with you, because of the habit.

After the first sergeant told us that he wanted us to inform him of any dope activities, he then told Ed and I that we were assigned to the 2nd platoon. Their location was the first bunker off to the right next to the front gate. We met the 1st Lieutenant in charge of the 2nd platoon.

He was a brother (African-American) from Philadelphia. His name was Lieutenant Johnson. There was twenty guys in this platoon including Ed and me. We met this guy who was a short-timer; his name was Robert Brown. They made Ed and me feel welcome.

Robert Brown just returned to the field after recovering from injuries received from a battle in September just when Ed and I arrived in Cu-Chi. Robert Brown had received injuries from scrapped metal to his back and legs. He walked with a limp until his leg wounds healed.

The other guy, a good friend of Robert Brown, who was Caucasian, also was wounded, with scrapped metal injuries to his back. He had more time left in the country than Robert Brown. But he would be out of Vietnam before Ed and me; his departure was in June of 1969. This tall blond-haired guy was named Rick. He looked like he played football, but he did not. However, Robert Brown played football for his high school. His position was tight end.

There was another brother named Lemon who wanted to leave Vietnam with $25,000–$40,000. He could, by playing dice, from the first until the middle of each month. The first of the month was pay day.

Lemon would take the convoy back into base camp Cu-Chi, just to play dice. He came up with some excuse so he could play dice to fulfill his dream to buy a package store. Lemon would ask several guys he knew to purchase money orders for him in order to mail $3,000–$4,000 to his mother so she could save it for him to buy his dream business.

You see, the largest money order amount any one person could buy in one month was $250, so Lemon had a lot of people buying money orders for him.

Ed and I started meeting some of the other guys and wanted to find out what was happening as far as action in the field; more or less, how dangerous it is out here. They said that this was a light duty assignment compared to the action they were in two weeks ago.

You see, God did not want Ed and me out here two weeks ago right after our training class. God wanted us to find out more about this combat thing by talking with these guys that are out here, with the heavy action. Thank you Lord, was all that Ed and I could say as we looked at each other, with some joy.

V

Who's the Funny Guy?

We continued talking. They were telling us what to do when you came under fire. So I said, That's not what we or at least I was told in Fort Pork. They said, So what? I played along and then they told us how to handle that type of a fire fight.

I said, The training center and Fort Pork told us to assault and keep firing. Robert Brown and Rick Pastal said, You keep using those assaults and you're going to be a dead brother. I answered, I'm not going to do that; I'm just telling you what the people told us. Everyone started laughing as I continued with my demonstration of training. They said, The first thing you do is get down to determine where the rounds are being fired from so you can return gunfire. You don't stand up and start assaulting because you cannot see Sir Charles. He's in the tree or underground or on the ground shooting knee high. This is one of the reasons you must get down or get behind something before you begin returning gunfire.

Then Robert Brown and Rick Pastal hit the note of survival; When you're fired upon, don't try to use all of those things you where taught in the training center and at Fort Pork from A.I.T, because you will not make it home. You must use your instincts to make it out of here. I knew they were right and they were serious in what they were telling Ed and me, and I was still trying to relax myself from the convoy ride.

Ed and I kind of looked around the location from where we stood and said, Well, we have 341 days left here. Lets make the best of them. Brown said, Look guys, don't try to be any hero; they don't make it home.

At about 6:00 P. M. the mail was handed out to all the platoons and the person assigned to Lieutenant Johnson platoon as radio telephone operator (RTO) distributed the mail. There was always a summary pack that arrived with the mail that contained chocolate bars, gum, cigarettes, matches, writing paper, pens, envelopes, shaving cream, razor blades, etc.; some basic things someone or group in the U.S. felt we needed.

Sometimes beer would arrive with the soda, but the beer was limited to two per person. Since I didn't drink or need it, I would give my beer and cigarettes to whoever wanted them. I prayed a lot to make it home. That's what I wanted, home.

That first day in the field, neither Ed nor I received any mail. The guys said, It takes about a month, you guys; meaning, Ed and I have about ten more days to wait if we don't get our heads blown off first with that training and Fort Pork (then Rick cursed).

I smiled, but had pains on the inside of my stomach. I guess Rick was mad about being in Vietnam more than he truly let on. You, see, Brown and Rick were married, but Rick said, Let's see how long you'll keep smiling when your old lady writes you a Dear John letter. I realized that Rick must be having some marital problems.

I said, When was the last time you saw your wife? He said, About two months ago in Hawaii; he was still thinking about that good time and was angry because his wife was 16,000 miles away from Vietnam. Sometimes loved ones in the States are afraid, too, because they can't do anything to protect you, so that's part of the reason more

31

women write Dear John letters to guys in combat.

The women at home are lonely and would be basket cases if they found out that their boyfriend or husband had been killed, so to ease the pain some of them cheat on their mate. I really do think women in the States didn't think at all about what effect a Dear John letter has on the guy they send the letter to.

Guys that receive Dear John letters become very dangerous to themselves and to the unit. What the soldier really wants to do, to his mate, is hurt her for waiting until he was over in Vietnam, before she became woman enough to tell him she wanted to be with someone else. It's sad how one can only think of oneself.

Anyway, Rick continued talking and said you know I want to make it home so my wife and I can have a baby. Rick had been married for about a year. They were married just before he entered the armed forces. Brown had two children, a boy and a girl, and said he might be home for Christmas this year. Many of the other guys started talking about home as well, but one could not forget.

That night it was very hard for me to think about closing my eyes. My thoughts were about Sir Charles and what this man could possibly do to anyone asleep.

Just then my eyes saw a figure that darted across the bunker entrance, walked in, and touched Rick, saying, you're on guard duty.

My heart settled down and I thought to myself that I must try to know who the enemy is and who is not. Everyone pulls guard duty for two hours each night; however, because this was Ed's and my first night in the fields, they passed us over. There were ten bunkers that were manned by our company and they always had to have someone pulling guard duty twenty-four hours a day.

Then morning came at five o'clock. Breakfast would be

served in a half an hour. So we got up and put some water in the metal part of our helmets so we could brush our teeth and wash our face and hands. Showers were available each day between 4:00 P.M. and 6:00 P.M.

Then you could turn in your dirty old fatigues to receive clean ones. After breakfast the bridge we were guarding would open up for travel. There were two towns joined by the Phu-Vinh bridge, where Sir Charles wanted to blow it up. Before the citizens could travel across this Phu-Vinh bridge, Alpha company would send out a team, to do mine sweeps on the road each morning.

This was done because during the night Sir Charles could have placed mines in the road to blow up our tanks and troops. This was also done for the safety of the citizens, for both sides of the Phu-Vinh bridge were swept.

There was a Calvary Division about two miles on the other side of the bridge, which was the closest small base camp if we needed to purchase items from the PX. Other convoys traveled over the bridge to other places in the area. It was very busy during the daylight hours. As the engines started, they went out the gate on their way to mine-sweep the road, Lieutenant Johnson volunteered Ed and me to join the mine-sweeping team.

This time Ed and I didn't act like we had, the day before, but the nervousness and blood pressure were present. We were told not to kick anything, rocks, cans, paper, bamboo sticks, or anything. You know, he didn't need to repeat that twice. I remembered everything he said.

Ed was on the left side of the road and I was on the right. Both of us were about fifty feet in front of the tanks, but seventy-five feet from the guys operating the mine sweepers. After about an hour and a half of walking, we had completed the mine sweep, but Ed and I watched the rice fields that were about fifty feet from the road on each side.

Was I afraid? You bet, but for some reason I felt more like a soldier on this day. My finger was on the trigger, my thumb on the switch to turn it from safety-lock to automatic. Not semi-automatic, but automatic.

As we walked, everything was quiet and we did not step off the road. There was a point man, and when we stopped, his mine detector indicated that there was a mine planted five feet in front of him. So we had the demo-man come up from the rear of the team. He walked up to where the two guys were sweeping the road.

The demo-man checked the spot, then placed a small charge and a short fuse there. Everyone ran behind the tanks before the charge exploded. We kept a watchful eye on the surroundings until we reached the check point.

The tankers remained at the check point all day until it was time to close the Phu-Vinh bridge for the night. Then the tank would be escorted back by 6:00 P.M. from the check point location by one of the four platoons from Alpha company.

This process went on until we had to leave the bridge. At about noon that day gunfire rang out in the town of Phu-Vinh. Our platoon, the 2nd platoon, was in a stand down (this is known as a rest period), so our Lieutenant received a call from the CP to take action. Little did the CP know that Lieutenant Johnson had told us to saddle up once we heard the gunfire and the RTO stated that we were departing (in code to our CP).

"He said Alpha 6 this is Alpha 2 over," The reply: "This is Alpha 6 over."

"This is Alpha 2 departing the Fox-trot-Fox-Trot Lema over (which means friendly front lines)." The reply; "Alpha 6 copy out." "Alpha 2 out."

We moved into the town Phu-Vinh very quietly; then the Viet Cong was spotted. Ed and I jumped so quickly, we forgot to start firing our weapons. This other guy was firing his weapon and said, Ed and Joe, turn around and start shooting over near the riverbank.

So we turned and put our weapons up, not seeing where we were firing. We fired off a few rounds. After about a five-minute exchange of gunfire and two hundred rounds short, everyone stopped shooting.

The Lieutenant ran over to where Ed and I were sitting. He asked if we were okay. Nervously we answered, Ah, we guess we are okay. The Lieutenant turned and said, Okay, let's get moving. Ed and I were so confused about what had just happened, no one said anything about whether they had got this Sir Charlie guy, and here we are standing up and walking. Couldn't he shoot us in our backs? Man, what is this?

I had to pull up the rear and I kept looking behind me. This was truly new to me and now, more afraid than I had realized, I just wanted to call out for my mother and father to help me.

Then seven to ten children ran up behind me very quietly. That made me jump out of my skin. I had switched my weapon from safety to automatic, and by God's grace, once I saw the children I switched it back to safety. It all happened so fast. I had tears in my heart and was very angry that these children ran after the platoon just after we had exchanged gunfire with the enemy.

One guy turned around and said, Oh, Joe, they just want some American C-ration. I didn't care what they wanted, they had better get away from me, because they were still following the platoon and I had already told those kids to get out of here. Then I thought, maybe one of them might have a booby trap on them. I stopped; so did the children.

I said, No-C-ration, so leave. I truly yelled at the children. They turned and ran. I then felt bad for doing that to those children. I could not provide what they needed, plus, they didn't know that I was a new guy that had just arrived to the fields and was new at this war and soldier stuff.

The children wanted some food. That stayed on my mind always. But as we started moving out of the town of Phu-Vinh, I saw Lieutenant Johnson talking to this Vietnamese lady. She looked beautiful. A thought popped into my mind; Is the Lieutenant working with the Viet Cong? No, he couldn't be. So I asked, Lieutenant, who's that young lady? He said, My friend and she washes my clothes too. I asked, Can you trust her? You know, this is a war and I plan to make it back home.

The Lieutenant said, Look, I know caution, but there are some real nice people here too. One day you can come to town with me. I said, Thank you, I think I'll be safe inside the camp parameter. Then the RTO said, Alpha 6, this is Alpha 2 over, asking permission to return to the Fox-Tot-Fox-Tot-Lema over. Alpha 6 replied, Alpha 6 copy, response Alpha 2 roger out.

Now, here comes the question: Hey Joe and Ed, how did you guys like your first fire fight, asked Rick. I said, Man, it's dangerous and I wasn't all that cool this time. I want to go home. Ed said me too. I said, too much, too much for me. Later that day the mail arrived and Ed and I finally received letters from our family and friends.

I received a letter from my step-mother, telling me how much she missed me and that my father had not said too much, only had you written the family? Your father loves you so much that he cannot talk about it. He is hurt, because you're over there.

The other letter was from my sisters, who said, We missed you. Keep your head down and don't be a hero if you can help it. Both my step-mother and my sisters stated that they were praying for my safety.

I thought only if they knew, if there was a way that I could get out of this country I would take it. Then there was a letter from a girl named Phyllis. She is Caucasian, but always hung out with a friend of my cousin, who was African-American.

Phyllis and I had talked a few times and I had seen her at a few dances, but nothing serious or heavy. She was a good person. But if you read her letter you would have thought we had something going on. We were all instructed to burn every letter after we had finished reading them.

This was done so that Sir Charles would not get his hands on the letters and write our family or friends and tell them we were dead or had been captured. This had happened to some other guys in the past.

After chow that evening, I took a shower and put on some clean clothes and wrote letters to my family and friends.

That night I had to pull guard duty from midnight to one o'clock in the morning. That was a long one-hour shift. During the day there are tall grass sticks; when it is dark they look like a person moving, especially when you're sleepy or the wind is blowing.

When an object didn't look too clear, I would look at it again with the star-light-scope (nighttime binocular), which allowed me to see during the night. The star-light-scope would cast a color of green which made it possible for us to see at night.

So if there was movement out in front or on either side you were able to detect it. Morning came and we had breakfast. The tanks had to be walked to their check point, but no one from our platoon walked with the tanks. It was third platoon honor today. Second platoon had to go out on patrol, into the other town, on the other side over the Phu-Vinh bridge.

There was a school and the children were in their classroom being taught by their teacher. Funny, there's a war and in the U.S. children didn't want to go to school, because they were tired of it. Other than the Civil War, the War of Independence and the American Indian War in the United States, there has never been a foreign war. I pray that there never will be one.

You know, Vietnam has been fighting this war for a very long time; since the 1800s. First France had control of this country, then Australia and now Communism controlling the northern part of Vietnam, but not the south. So this civil war goes on.

Back to the school: The schoolteacher was very pretty and I spoke to her as we marched past her, going up the hill to check out the village area. We must have patrolled a five-mile area location and found no Viet Cong in the area. We returned to the camp location with our radio message as a standard policy for departure and returning.

VI

The RTO

Later that evening I started having hot and cold chills. I had caught malaria. Even though everyone took malaria tablets, you can still get it. It was not serious, requiring hospitalization care, but it was really bad just the same.

The guys took turns all night putting the blankets on and taking them off me as I became hot or cold. The day before, the Lieutenant had asked me if I wanted to become his radio operator, but I said I would think about it, because I had been informed by the instructor that Sir Charlie always shot the radio operator first. This way the platoon or company would not be able to call for support from any artillery or mortar battery station. So the next morning after getting up from a sleepless night, with a malaria fever, I went to eat breakfast, still weak from the malaria fever, trying to gain my strength by eating.

The Lieutenant approached me that morning and I said that I was not feeling well. He said, Unless you're wounded everyone saddle up, let's move out. He said, Oh Joe, do you want to be my RTO? Then I said, Yes, I'll try it. So I called the CP, Alpha 6 this is Alpha 2 over, reply, Alpha 6, respond, Alpha 6 over, Alpha 2, asking permission to leave the Fox-trot-Fox-trot-lema, reply, Alpha 6 copy, response Alpha 2 out.

This radio weighted twenty-five pounds, plus I had my M–16 (9.25 lbs.), 20 magazines (3.75 lb. each), and two, two-quart canteens of water. I had about 125 lbs. on my back as we patrolled the area and I was not aware of how far we were going on this day.

As we walked, we were ten to fifteen feet apart from each man. This would reduce Sir Charles's chances of shooting all of us. This was a very hot, trying day for me. I could see the heat bounding off the trees; however, there was a breeze that cooled us as we walked through the fields. I was tired, so we stopped about noontime to eat our C-rations and rest up before marching ahead.

We knew a little about everybody by just talking with each another about our lives. We depended upon each other to defeat Sir Charles. This recon patrol had another light day, as we walked through the canals which were known to have leeches in the water.

However, we made it through the canals without picking up any leeches. Normally they attached themselves to our clothes. We have started back to the Alpha company camp site. We all talked a lot about things. I guess nervous energy, due to our environment.

I am not a hero, just afraid, so we all needed to fire our weapons to survive. Every man, African-American and Caucasian, treated each other with respect; each man as his brother and friend. We needed each other badly out here.

We talked about girlfriends, church, and what some of the guys did at home. We sang a church song, but hummed them so it would not be so loud when we were on patrol. We didn't want Sir Charles to hear us.

We contacted the CP so they would not fire their weapons upon us by mistake, as we entered the parameter. I called and asked permission to enter the Fox-Trot-Trot-Lema. You could hear the grenades that were thrown into the river water from the bunker located under the bridge. They exploded Bom-Bom-Bom, as we entered the gates.

We continue with our patrolling and as the time was

passing I decided to have my picture taken standing on the Phu-Vinh bridge. The daylight has always been a good sight to see each morning, thanking God for each day that He allows us to see. I now have 329 days left in the country.

As for the nighttime, you can keep it, you can't see anything in front of you at all and that's dangerous. It has been said, that some platoons and Sir Charles bumped into each other one night. No one fired their weapons; everyone just ran because they didn't know who they should shoot.

Sometimes at night we would shoot off flares that would illuminate the night sky, to see the area in front of our bunker, to see if there was any movement by Sir Charles. The CP always had a light on, which made it easy to walk over to the mess hall. It was located at a distance and would have been a very dark area, if the light was not left on to locate the CP.

The next time the tanks went out, Ed and I had to walk point. Man, I didn't need this honor, to be the first one to be shot. That's what normally happens to the point men: They're shot first on a patrol.

So Ed and I got ready for action this time. Now we had a few days under our belts so we were not as nervous, and didn't have our blood pressure increase as much as it had in the past.

We were told that before we arrived, two other guys walked point and one guy saw a can and kicked it. It blew his foot off. I said, no cans or anything else will be kicked by me today. Ed took the left side and I was on the right. We proceeded up the paved road. I began to think of my strategy and other things that might take place, as far as what would I do if Sir Charles popped out of nowhere.

If Sir Charles come from the front, on the side, what about if my weapon jams, should I use hand-to-hand combat, or if they start firing their weapons, will I survive the attack? The more I thought about the possible encounters, the more my stomach felt like butterflies.

As I moved forward, I kept thinking, don't kick cans, don't step on the grass that may be elevated a little more than the rest, watch out, if the grass is brown it may be booby trapped. Don't, Don't, Don't, step watch this, watch that, watch, please stop! I'm cool.

This walk was the pressure that could break the tough guys that were in the street gangs. Any men that wanted to be bad, here's your chance. This was not in the streets at home where your buddies had your backs, in Nam you better be cool, smooth, and twice as quick or you're dead.

I felt like those cartoons, you know, when the cat eyes circle through his head, that's what my eyes did as I checked out everything. I felt like I had three pairs of eyes watching everything as I walked. As the tightness in my stomach slackened, a cold sweat dropped from my forehead.

"As I called unto the Lord to help my footsteps, help me not to freeze, where I'm not able to fire this weapon, watch over this team sweeping this road that we are kept safe. Oh, Lord, help us right now father in Jesus' name. Amen."

I felt much better after this prayer. I looked around and noticed that we had not traveled that far from the bunkers and had a way to go on this two and a half mile mine sweep. It was also a little cloudy out this morning and more people appeared to have been in the rice fields than usual, but we marched forward, as I reaffirmed my faith in God with each step and breath I took.

I was angry at myself for being in Vietnam, wondering what I had done to be in this country. Where I have been under pressure, I arrived to Vietnam knowing that I was coming out to the field. And now it is no longer just a thought of what might happen when I get to Vietnam. I said, I'm here now; it's the thought, will I ever make it home.

Pressure. Do you really understand what real pressure is like? I do and it's not fun at all. I felt like crying, dying, yelling, beating up the congressmen, and disappearing all at once.

You see, the thoughts of family now were put on hold. The thoughts of a girlfriend was placed on hold. You had to become a jungle type of a person, an animal type for smelling, with a hunger for wanting to live; holding onto God, that's it, you and Sir Charles. But he was better in many ways than we were in this country; this was this man's home.

Because your life was not year-to-year or month-to-month, nor day-to-day, or hour-to-hour, you may have felt that you lost all of that precious time just to settle for life to be minute-by-minute. In one second a bullet could take your life. Oh, I was afraid. You just don't know how this pressure wiped the heart of life for living from me.

This was torture that troubles every man's mind, but through it all every man had prepared himself for death in one form or another. But a bitter fight would take place to the end: no one wanted to be shot and killed by a sniper's bullet. We all wanted to go down fighting, if it had to happen.

We arrived at the check point where the tanks would remain until 6:00 P.M. each evening. We then rode back to the bridge site on the truck.

We all talked about our feelings; this was a form of therapy for us, so no one would be too uptight if we were under fire or if one received a Dear John letter. Everyone was very protective of everyone else, which was pretty cool.

But there was always one that wanted to demonstrate

that he had more courage than the rest. That's the one you watch out for. He might lead the platoon into an ambush, so he can play hero. He wants medals and honor. I had told many guys not to mess up because I plan to go home. So they better be cool, when I'm on patrol with them.

Later that morning we went on a helicopter ride, which we called a chopper (also known as a eagle flight). The helicopters landed on the road with our bunkers on each side of the road that went across the Phu-Vinh bridge. All of Alpha company boarded. The helicopter's flight was my first eagle flight. This was in the month of October, 1968.

We were flying into a hot landing zone (LZ), meaning that gunfighting was going on as we boarded the choppers in the area that we were being flown to. We had to get out of the chopper very quickly and start returning gunfire as soon as we touched the ground; no time to wait.

On this mission there were four helicopters as a mobile air unit. As we lifted up into the sky and as it took off, you could hear the chopping sound made by the propellers of the helicopter. There were two Cobra gun ships, helicopters that escorted us to the hot LZ. Then the Cobra choppers went on ahead of us to prep the area, so we could land into the battle area.

This prepping is done when the Cobra gun ships fire rockets, automatic machine gun rounds, and grenade rounds upon the LZ area we were landing in. This would be done to keep the enemy down, under cover, and off of us so we could land. Then the choppers would come down and drop us off so that we would be able to return gunfire at Sir Charles. It was a quick deplane from the helicopters so that the choppers would not be shot down.

The noise level from the helicopters made it hard to give direction once we deplaned from the helicopter. So we used sign language to do the speaking for us. The runner on the helicopter was about twelve feet from the ground because of the water. The pilot did not know how deep the water would be, so we had to jump from that height to the water.

Once on the ground we started returning gunfire. When I jumped out of the helicopter, the radio bunched up then down on my back. Oh boy, that hurt, but it was comfortable because my thoughts were on this mission and what other kinds of pain I would receive if I didn't get out of the way of Sir Charles's bullets.

As we started our sweep of the area, you could see purple smoke that was dropped from the gun ship to mark the area that we should land in. There was other smoke from the rounds fired from the AK–47 rifles, the weapon Sir Charles used against us, along with the smoke of M–16 gunfire.

The time was about 9:00 A.M. as we continued moving in the direction where Sir Charles was spotted. Our company had the back door for another company in this battle, putting Sir Charles in the middle.

The plan was to box Sir Charlie in and take him out. We spread out in our sweep, moving with caution to get Sir Charles and at the same time having all soldiers return to the camp safely. Caution, caution, each step we took was slow, and the hot sun was great as we moved through the bamboo tree line and the thick brush where booby traps best hide.

As we moved through the thick brush and had to make it to a clearing, where a village stood, we employed much more caution, because this could become a battle ground.

There appears to have been movement detected, but it was just our minds and nothing else. I communicated over the radio with the instruction received from the Lieutenant of our platoon to the other platoons, letting them know that every move must be made very quietly. The sweep would cover an area of about ten clicks (ten miles). This was a long way to carry over one hundred pounds on your back in the heat.

To keep myself from becoming too thirsty and tired, I drank very little water and placed a small pebble under my tongue to keep my mouth moist. This was my first forced march so I recalled some things from my training in Fort Pork, that I felt might help me out here. With the radio, ammo, canteens of water, and the M–16, I started sweating after about two plus miles, with prayer always on my lips.

VII

The New Lieutenant

The sun stood directly in the sky, allowing all the heat to come down upon us. Pre-plan for a schedule departure was in another location. We had to be there by 3:00 P.M. or spend the night out here in the field. Thank God there wasn't any activity that day and we all returned to our camp site safely.

We were told once we returned to our camp area that we would be eagle flown on the other side of the area we patrolled today. The intelligence section of our battalion in Vietnam said that it had been reported that there was heavy VC (Viet Cong) movement in this area. Alpha company's mission would be to stop the movement of VC troops.

That night I had the first watch on guard duty. I was on the top of the bunker looking out, scanning the area in front of our bunker by sight and the star-light-scope. I had thought that I saw movement, so I looked again through the star-light-scope. Then a trip flare went off. I picked up my M-16 and got down, pointing my weapon in the direction that the trip flare had gone off, I sent up a hand flare to illuminate the area, then we sighted it.

It was a jack rabbit. Before I became aware of what it was, my heart was just throbbing, not knowing if the VC was out in front of my bunker.

Each watch was for two hours and yet, within that two hours' time, the whole world could end. We always inform the next man that pulls guard duty what happened on our watch. I never gave any thought to time prior to coming to Vietnam. I never knew how short life was before, I said to myself.

While in the U.S., my plans were to retire from some company. Now I might not have that opportunity; here one minute and your life is over the next minute. No, I didn't hang onto life; I started living my life for the first time knowing how short it could be.

I had no time to remain upset at the military because they sent me to Vietnam; but to learn how to enjoy life in Vietnam, so I did. Ed had the next watch so I woke him, but I explained what happened during my guard watch.

The next morning everyone was up at 6:00 A.M. for chow. The Phu-Vinh bridge was not a bad assignment compared to other assignments my company could have been on. We were still able to take showers every day; that was good compared to the remainder of my tour of duty. Also having a change of clean clothes was important because of the heat and rain you found yourself in throughout the day. Sweaty clothes left an odor in your clothes until you showered.

This Phu-Vinh bridge assignment ended in November of 1968. So we planned the mission for this next eagle flight, which was further on the other side of Phu-Vinh where there was more movement, next to the canals, in the swamp area. Oh, leeches!!

We were walking in the canals. There were red ants walking on a banana leaf so I moved away so the ants would not get on me. These ants jumped from the leaf onto my radio as I was inserting a plastic bag over the phone piece, which you speak through, to prevent water from wetting the hand-set.

I then lifted my M–16 up to keep it from getting wet, so it would be operational when I needed it. I had received this advice from the guys that had been in-country longer than I.

We searched the canal for weapons that day. The canal would have been a good place for the VCs to store their weapons. If there was heavy VC movement in this area they would need to hide their weapons to provide cover for themselves. They could use these weapons later, so they pretended to be farmers.

The ants from the leaf that landed on my radio began moving up to my neck, biting me. I began to hit the ants and the guy behind me started brushing the ants off the radio. I pulled the other three ants off my neck. They were bored in my neck. Ouch! Boy! They stung me, just like a bee had stung. Swelling appeared immediately on my neck and the medic gave me some medicine for the bites.

There were leeches in the canal, but a few other guys and I placed the bottom part of our fatigues in our boots before we entered the canal. So when you enter the water, air pockets develop, blowing up your fatigues. This will prohibit the leeches from sucking on the part of your body that's in the water.

When you're out of the water, you're able to brush the leeches off your clothes because they did not attach themselves to your skin. We would tie our shirts too, to keep the leeches from attaching themselves to our bodies to suck our blood. The water was waist high as we walked through the canal. I did not see any more red ants swimming on the water as we continued searching the canal for the VC's weapon storage.

Because I was Lieutenant Johnson's RTO (Radio Transmission Operator) I was close to him as we walked through the canal. He was telling me that he sang with this group in Philadelphia, but it was a local group in his area. The Lieutenant said, however, he did have a nice voice. From that point the Lieutenant and I started to build a friendship, partly because I was his RTO.

I did all the transmission over the phone radio. I would give the grid cores (Latitude and Longitude) for pick up and C-ration drops, and indicate to the CP, grid cores for artillery drops or mortar round drops. Even though the radio was heavy all of the time, it was nice to do something of importance. If I didn't know how to read a map or understand how to operate the radio, I would not have been the Lieutenant's RTO.

As the Lieutenant and I continued talking he told me that he was married and had two children, a boy and girl in the U.S. I didn't say anything.

On mission, if we did not reach our pick-up location in time to be eagle-flown back to our camp site, we had to walk back if it was possible or sleep out there for the night.

We came out of the canal wet from our waist down, pumping water out of our boots through the air holes on the insides of the arches. Smelling like water buffalo as the heat from the sun started to dry our fatigues, we walked quickly to find cover.

There was a village next to the canal area, because the water from the canal was used to irrigate the rice fields for these farmers. With caution we approached the village and noticed that there were men, old men. Most men were considered to be VC, if not part of the Vietnamese army. My question was, why were these men there?

This village had signs that it had been hit by U.S. artillery or VC rockets. Some of the children and the older people received injuries from the explosion of this artillery or rocket attack. Our medic or doc looked at a few of the people in the village to see if he was able to do anything for them.

Everyone in the village that was twelve years or older had to have an ID card. The ID card would tell us the age of that person, if they were male, and if they were between the ages of fourteen and forty-five. You would be either in the Vietnamese army or considered to be a Viet Cong.

In the village that day there were not any surprises that were sprung on us, just some sad village people I guess trying to figure out how they could stop the pain and go on with their lives. I just looked and as we took a break to eat our C-rations, I reflected on my family and wondered what they would say if they saw me now.

We kept the C-ration cans, because if we threw them away the VC would make a booby trap out of them, to be used to kill us.

We left this village area and marched back to our company camp area on the Phu-Vinh bridge. Once we arrived to our camp location I called our company CP. "Alpha 6 this is Alpha 2 over—this is Alpha 6 copy—Alpha 2 asking permission to enter the Fox-trot-Fox-trot-Lima over—Alpha 6 copy, Alpha 2, you have permission, roger—Alpha 6, Alpha 2 roger that over and out, Alpha 6 roger out."

The rest of the company on the bunker line were watching to see if the second platoon was approaching the front gate. If not, were they ready to blow away the group that would enter the gate? Then they saw us walking down the street, tired, hungry, dirty, and not smelling too great, but the rest of the platoons were glad to see us march back into the camp.

The Lieutenant and I, after we showered and put on clean clothes, went to the Phu-Vinh town. We took our weapons and went to this Vietnamese lady's house that the Lieutenant knew. She had always washed the Lieutenant's clothes and he would pay her with M.P.C. (Military Payment Currency). This day, as we walked, I was a little more relaxed, but ready for any action if there was any.

This lady asked us in and hugged the Lieutenant. I put

two and two together, and said to myself, this must be a whore house, but I was wrong. This lady liked, and was in love with, the Lieutenant, and he told me on our way back that he loved her. Then I said, What about your wife and children in Philadelphia. He said that he was not going to take this Vietnamese lady back to the U.S.

Then he said, I'm going to marry her so that I will not catch any diseases from the women in this country; I will be just with her. He wanted me to meet one of her friends. I said, No thank you, and we went back to the base camp.

Later that week, the Lieutenant and the Vietnamese lady were married, but he would only be able to see her during daylight hours, because the VC normally came into the town at night and the gates are closed at first dark. Then Lieutenant Johnson was transferred to the 3rd platoon and 2nd platoon received another Lieutenant, named Robert Nebask.

During this time I met this Arvin soldier who taught me to speak some Vietnamese. Every night I would get with him to have a class to understand different words to make a sentence in the Vietnamese language. I would write something in English and he would write it in Vietnamese to help me to understand the word and how it sounded.

It was very beneficial when we met many different people in the village and there were Vietnamese young ladies in the village and in the towns. When we were able to communicate with the Vietnamese people a little bit, it helped them become comfortable with us, and us with them. Knowing some parts of the language was important.

There were other troops that arrived with this new Lieutenant that day, which were assigned to 3rd and 4th platoon. I met this other brother named Stucky. I knew it was not his real name, but that was all he said, Call me Stucky, man.

I never saw Stucky; he never went out on patrol with us, but this day they wanted me to pull guard duty under the bridge, because Stucky was taking the convoy into Cu-Chi. Stucky told me that I would need to throw these percussion grenades in the Phu-Vinh river every fifteen to twenty minutes. This was done to prevent the VC from swimming down river and blowing up the bridge. If we did not exercise this type of security Sir Charles would blow the bridge up. I did not like this at all. I said to myself, a grenade can blow up in my hand, then no more Joseph.

So I started throwing the grenades in the water. I was a little nervous, with these grenades, because it could have a shorter fuse than normal and explode in my hand and kill me. When I threw one of the grenades, it slipped after I released the handle, so I threw that one very quickly. It appeared that it exploded as it hit the surface of the water and did not explode beneath the water. That was a short fuse; normally you have a three-second count, before you throw the grenade.

Stucky also smoked dope and ask me if I wanted some. I told him no, so he said, you're not going to tell the First Sergeant on me. I said, No man, just be cool with the stuff so no one gets killed because you're high, man.

As Stucky left for Cu-Chi, I continued throwing these grenades in the water to bring up Sir Charles if he was in the water, dead or alive. I pulled this bridge patrol for three days. It wasn't too bad, but the part I liked was that I did not go out on mission with my platoon.

After pulling guard duty under the bridge these few days, I met another Arvin soldier who I asked to teach me Vietnamese. He said that he would. When night had come, Lieutenant Nebask assigned me to pull guard duty on this other bunker near the bridge, so I went.

I felt it was all right talking to the Vietnamese people

during the day, but how could I trust this Arvin soldier at night? I felt that they could be a VC and come out once it was night. He might cut my throat if I fell asleep. So the Arvin soldier that pulled guard duty with me on the bunker was the soldier that I had asked to teach me Vietnamese earlier that day.

I felt good knowing that I could write words or some sentence in English and he would write the sentence in Vietnamese and pronounce each word to me. I had ask him how you said, what is your name—water—ice water—ID, then he would spell the words for me.

The other Arvin soldier did not speak English that well and it was hard learning his language from him. So I was learning the basics that I needed while in Vietnam.

This training session went on for about three weeks. I enjoyed it and applied it, when we went out on patrol mission. So in some sense of all that was going on, the Arvin soldier and I became friends.

There was a blend of different levels of educated people in our company and platoon. There were teachers, college students, factory workers, businessmen, playboys, etc., that made up this man's army. In other words, there was a great deal of intelligence in the jungle. You would think that was the case at all times, in a third-world country like Vietnam, but our common sense sometimes did not kick in on time.

We had this other guy in our platoon named Robert. He is a schoolteacher. He was waiting to hear from his wife whether they had had their baby yet. He was an oddball person, with his thinking in the field.

He looked like a well-educated person, but needed to be reminded about caution with his weapons, like keeping the safety switch in the off position. On your weapon until you need to use it, you leave the grenade pin in until you needed it. The guy was nice, but too dangerous to be around in the jungle.

Robert was pulling guard duty under the bridge one night with a Vietnamese soldier. Robert pulled the grenade pin out to throw the grenade, but he threw it too high up inside of the bunker. The grenade bounced off the top part of the bunker and rolled under the hammock, where the Vietnamese soldier was sleeping, but Robert called him in time so that when it exploded, Robert was on the outside of the bunker and the Vietnamese soldier was on his way out of the bunker.

The Vietnamese soldier was not killed, but was seriously wounded from the scrapped metal of the grenade after it exploded. Everyone asked themselves, Why did Robert throw the grenade from inside of the bunker, when everybody throws the grenades standing on the outside of the bunker. This incident took place around the end of October 1968.

Nothing was done to Robert, but he was reassigned to Cu-Chi, to work in the supply room. He stayed in the field until his orders were cut. He heard from home: he and his wife had a baby boy. This reassignment may have been good for him so he could relax and think about his family.

Mail call, that was my responsibility, as the RTO. I called everyone by his first name. I made a mistake and called our new Lieutenant Robert and not Lieutenant Nebask. He was on my back quick.

I told him that it would not happen again, but many of the guys started cursing___and said, We are all out here together and we don't have____anytime to be calling___you all of that. I told the guys, That's okay, the Lieutenant is new and he may change later if time permits.

I told the Lieutenant that he should forget the training he received from Panama. It is different from any training received from America, keep low and be cool. He told me to be cool, as he's the officer in charge and will be giving the orders.

I sat down to open my mail that I received from Phyllis and my family with a smile on my face. Little did the Lieutenant know that the body count was very high among lieutenants that were too pushy. They had a habit of catching an M–16 round in the back of the head. Dead they were.

I had taken a picture on the Phu-Vinh bridge and sent it home to my sister Jannie. She still has it, with some of the other pictures that I sent to her awhile back.

I told Lieutenant Nebask that I was the RTO, but he was still upset because he felt that I had more control over the platoon than he did.

So I said, Look, if you expect to make it out here for the next six months, you have to do your job and forget about spit shine boots and the troops saluting you. Our main objective is to return home alive, not to deal with form and what's fashionable.

We are soldiers fighting a war. We are not in any parade. Then Lieutenant Nebask said, If your attitude remains the same you will be court martialed. I said, If you do I will have three hot meals a day, with clean clothes and showers. The Lieutenant looked at me turned pink, and walked away.

The next day we had an eagle flight, to recon this area that was reported to have heavy VC activity. Once the helicopters arrived at the location, the gun ships that flew ahead of us started prepping the landing zone.

Lieutenant Nebask did not want to get out of the chopper because there was water and the chopper propellers were blowing the water along. The height the chopper was hovering at, made it difficult to jump.

One of the gunners on the chopper started pushing the

Lieutenant out of the chopper door, because the chopper was now a sitting duck for Sir Charles to shoot down. The gunner yelled and pushed the Lieutenant again so he would get out of the chopper.

The Lieutenant hit the water with a belly flop from the gunner's push. I jumped into the water and grabbed the Lieutenant, because he was acting like the water was deeper than four feet. He was totally wet, mad, afraid, and yelling out to the chopper, Wait!

I asked if he was okay and he turned quickly and walked away. He started shouting and we told him to keep it down, you are going to give your direction using sign language. He looked at the faces of twenty men and said Yes, and I didn't mean to yell.

As we moved out from the landing area slowly, we found many booby traps. I signaled for the demo man to set charges to explode these booby traps. None of the booby traps were set off until the platoon was a distance away from that area. Then it would explode, blowing up the booby traps.

We were told initially that this would be a hot LZ so as we proceeded with our recon through the hedged roll we were then fired upon by the VC. We hit the ground and opened fire. After a burst of our fire power we waited for about five minutes, then we closed in on the area.

The VC sniper just shot a few rounds off and fled from the area, leaving his sandal behind as he ran down the trail from our burst of fire power.

We followed the trail where the VC left his sandals, to see where it was going to lead us. The trail led us to a village and we began asking mama-san if she or anyone had seen the VC that just fired the weapon and ran in this direction of the village. They said no, no one came this way. We began searching the village to see if the VC was there.

We saw a bunker area, which we approached with caution.

A couple of guys threw grenades in the bunkers, not knowing if the VC had hidden in there or not. Then it was checked out for bodies or weapons. We did not find anything in that bunker. Then we went over to the water buffalo pit and checked it as well.

We came up empty from our search of the VC and the weapons that were used to shoot at us and he ran off to another location underground that the village people would not tell us, or did not know of, because they feared for their lives. What can one truly say to these people in this country? They lived there, we were just visiting for awhile.

We moved out of the village to complete our recon in order to meet the choppers at the place of pick-up in time. One could only wonder how close were we to this VC.

This recon sweep was a very short one, about three miles from the landing LZ to the pick-up location. We returned to the camp site and relaxed, having our super, then reading our mail.

There have been times when I have used my ration card to purchase cigarettes and beer for the guys. Initially I was not going to do it, but I gave in and asked God to forgive me. I did not drink nor did I smoke anything. The purchases were made at another base camp, which had a PX store to purchase items. We went from the end of September to November on the bridge duty. It was a nice location with a few patrols,. This was nice too, we ate, showered, had clean clothes, and received our mail on time, while on this type of duty. I would like to have done this duty until September 1969, without any injuries if it was possible.

I'm not worrying, I told myself, because I had a place inside of the wire each night. Unbeknownst to us, this good time would turn into rough times. This happened around

November 2, 1968. The time was about 3:00 A.M.

I had just completed my guard watch and awakened Ed about 2:00 A.M. and when he got up I laid down in his hammock.

Then it happened. Boom!, boom!, boom!, boom!, boom!, the sound of mortars or rockets exploding, flares being shot off. We all jumped up, then a larger explosion went off as we heard the machine guns and M–16 gunfire.

We saw the tank on the Phu-Vinh bridge slide off into the Phu-Vinh river. Lieutenant Nebask, ran up to the CP and discovered that two VCs had swum down the Phu-Vinh river and threw a saco charge at the Phu-Vinh bridge, which blew up one side of the bridge.

The guys in the bunkers under the bridge threw multiple percussion grenades into the water, killing one VC, but the other VC managed to throw his saco charge, which blew the bridge. From that saco charge explosion, the scrapple metal killed the Captain, First Sergeant, one Cook, and one Lieutenant. Several other troops were wounded.

That's when all the shooting started. The other soldiers were shooting at the other VC swimming in the water with their M–16s, and the M–60 machine gunfire. They finally shot and killed the other VC.

Because of all the commotion, no one thought to ask about the soldier that always slept under the tank each night, which had fallen into the Phu-Vinh river off of the Phu-Vinh bridge. After about an hour, the wounded and the dead were medic-vac to the hospital by helicopter back to Cu-Chi.

Then everyone began asking about the soldier that slept under the tank. Where is he? The radio transmission operator called Cu-Chi headquarters requesting for drivers to search for the soldier's body that went down in the Phu-Vinh river with the tank.

The divers arrived about 7:00 A.M. that morning. There were four divers, diving all day in shifts; but they were not able to locate the body, they said, because the tank was stuck in the mud on the bottom of the river, which made it hard to locate the body.

Then they had a crane arrive that next day and the divers returned to the river. This river was also very dirty and had strong undercurrents, the divers said as they approached the bottom. The crane was not able to lift the tank out of the river, but it lifted the tank high enough so that the divers were able to see if the soldier's body was under the tank, with their underwater flashlights.

There was no one under the tank, they said, and that it was possible that the current washed the body out into the larger body of the river that leads into the sea.

For four days they tried to remove the tank from the bottom of the Phu-Vinh river. They had a crane helicopter and two cranes on the river bank. This tank could not be moved.

VIII

The Wolfhounds Claim Victory

Two days after the blowing off the bridge, some engineers arrived and began building a pontoon bridge. This allowed the army supply trucks and the local townspeople to travel from one town to the next.

With all the activity that was going on, due to the bridge blowing up one platoon remained trapped on the other side of the Phu-Vinh bridge.

There was a particle walkway that was usable and the other platoon was able to use it, but they had to proceed with caution as they crossed the bridge. The bridge was supported with one support beam that could fall at any time if there was too much weight.

We remained at this site until the 11th of November. Because we had allowed Sir Charles to blow the bridge, we were to be reassigned other duty. Well the honeymoon (the bridge duty) was over and, not knowing what our next duty assignment would be, all we could think of was battle ground action for sure.

Then replacements were sent to guard the other end of the bridge in order that the platoon that was trapped would be able to get some food and rest.

We met with the Arvin army Captain and other officers that indicated that they would help us guard the bridge by sending additional Arvin soldiers (Vietnamese soldiers) later to us in that day.

But we went to Vietnam to help the Vietnamese soldiers and people (South Vietnam), fight this battle against the Viet Cong (North Vietnam), not for South Vietnam to look at this war like it's ours and they were there to help us out. That's the way it felt the whole time, while being there.

Then there were Arvin soldiers, paratroops that were jumping from the plane. When they spotted VC moving across the rice fields, the paratroops parachuted from the plane, looking like clouds of mushrooms as they landed into a hot LZ. We could hear the gunfire and the firing of artillery, mortar rounds exploding as we viewed the clouds of mushrooms fall from the sky. Seeing the parachute, hearing the explosion, it was real as the battle grew stronger.

We still did light patrols in the Phu-Vinh area until Delta company replaced us (Alpha company) on the bridge. Then we left the Phu-Vinh bridge never to return to this place and went into Cu-Chi, our base camp for a two-day stand down (two days of rest and resupplies).

During the stand down we were to receive a new Captain, First Sergeant, another Lieutenant for fourth platoon, another cook, another medic, and a few more soldiers to replace those that were wounded and had not fully recovered.

This was a disgrace to the Wolfhounds, Sir Charles blew up the bridge, so now the Wolfhounds had to restore their name and reclaim themselves as the victor. Man, Ed and I were so glad that neither he nor I had not gotten hurt, we could have cared less about the Wolfhound's name. I'm alive, that's what really counts.

By the time we had arrived at Cu-Chi we felt that the blowing up of the bridge was all over the base camp. Many of the Caucasian soldiers were fighting mad and wanted to kill Sir Charles just for the shame of the Wolfhounds.

We managed to get everyone to cool down and told them that we were to enjoy this stand down for a couple of days, so let's do that, and get cleaned up to do the town. You heard a loud yell. All right, we said, and hit the showers.

This stand down had supplied Alpha company with ninety cases of beer and twenty cases of soda. Those that drank beer tried their best to drink all ninety cases. I was a soda drinker, because it had been said that Sir Charles has also entered our base camp on occasion.

That night the company had an entertainment show for us, a song and dance group. It was not well known, but we enjoyed the music anyhow. This had been the only live entertainment we had seen or heard over here. This party began by 6:00 P.M. that evening and by 11:00 P.M. that night we had many drunk and sick GIs, including Ed.

I brought Ed back to the barracks. He was real sick. Ed wanted to throw up so I walked him to the screen door of the barracks. He leaned to the side of the barracks to bring it up, and I put him in my famous bear hug. With this one tight squeeze, everything came up. Then I opened the screen door to the barracks, and walked Ed back to his bunk as he fell to the bunk on his back.

Many of the other guys assigned to the same barracks also made a stop at the front door to throw up before they entered the barracks. Some made it into the barracks and threw up on their bunks; some did not return because they could not walk back to the barracks, and others I helped in the door and helped some of them to throw up. Oh, what a night these guys had. Just wait until morning, I said to myself, they are going to be sorry for all this drinking.

The next morning, Ed complained of having sore ribs and thought that someone had beat him up. I told him what happened and Ed said, Next time don't squeeze me like that again. I said, Okay Ed, just learn how to hold your drinks and not be so sick. So we had to laugh and joke about it, then went to get some clean fatigues and clean our weapons. We did as much as possible, because we had no idea where this assignment would be and it's always better to be ready than to be unprepared.

We had time to read our mail and to send our letters, in order that they were mailed before we left Cu-Chi for our reassignment.

About 9:00 A.M. the new captain told us that we would be moving out by noon. Everyone asked what happened to the other day we should have off, but no one answered. We started packing our gear and other items that we felt were needed for this new assignment. We had about three hours to kill or two hours because we would need to be in formation with our gear by 11:00 A.M. for roll call.

Ed and I walked around Cu-Chi. We stopped at the PX and got a soda, then continued our walking from place to place, talking to some of the brothers from our company's station inside of Cu-Chi. It must have been around ten-forty-five by then, so Ed and I hurried back to our company headquarters.

As we saddled up to get on the convoy, the roll call was done and we stood in formation leaving our ranks to get on the truck. As our names were called, we boarded the trucks heading for another field camp, which was built by engineers. It was called Diamond II.

Diamond II was about six miles from Cu-Chi. I took life very seriously and my approach required caution. Our company had about 150 soldiers compared to my stateside company in basic training, which was about 250–275 soldiers; and our platoon was about 20–30 soldiers, compared to our stateside platoon of 70–80 soldiers.

Bravo company from our battalion was stationed at Diamond II, but had very little success pinpointing where the rockets were fired from in order to return artillery or mortar rounds fire back to the VC.

Diamond II was known to have been rocked at least three times per day and no one was able to stop Sir Charles from doing this in the past three months. So this is where Alpha company is going to be stationed to help locate Sir Charles and put him out of business. Both companies Alpha and Bravo were Wolfhounds. This was really trouble for the Viet Cong, but he did not know it yet. I guess you can say that Bravo and Alpha companies switched duty station so Alpha company could re-focus themselves for the job at hand.

Each evening we were told Sir Charles would send his rockets and mortar rounds into the Diamond II base camp, sometime over shooting the parameter, other times hitting a target and killing an American GI.

We filled sand bags as we built our bunkers. Later that evening, around 9:00 P.M., the rockets were launched by Sir Charles, hitting a tree a hundred feet behind our bunker as it shot scrapped metal everywhere. There were trees in the parameter that Sir Charles used as a marker to direct the launching of their rockets.

That night, as the barrage of rockets and mortars hit the camp, they were close. I was sitting on the bunker when the first rocket landed and exploded about a hundred feet from our bunker.

I moved very quickly into our bunker, faster than even the guys that were sitting in front of the bunker doorway. They entered the bunker after I went into bunker. Yes, I moved very fast when the action started.

Sir Charles was very good with the use of his weapon, with the launching of the rockets and mortar rounds into our artillery bays. They did not assault the camp site, but just peppered our location and I was glad that they did not assault us, because the nine of us left our weapons outside of the bunker.

I quickly realized that I had no weapon after I had entered the bunker and wanted to go back out to get mine. But the two guys next to the bunker opening were able to reach their weapons and told the rest of us that if anything happened they would let us know so that we can receive our weapons.

Then the barrage of rockets and mortars stopped and we re-surfaced. After looking at the trees behind us, I began thanking God for being yet still alive.

The sergeant over our mortar platoon was an African-American who stood about six-two and was built from the weights he lifted daily. During this attack he managed to view the flashes from the rockets and mortar, and where they were being launched from.

After the firing stopped he had the mortar platoon redirect their mortar tubes and returned a few mortar rounds in those two locations. Yes, he could have caught scrapped metal from the rockets and mortar rounds that landed in our parameter. That was the only way one could have determined where the rockets and mortars were being launched from.

Also, we found out that Lieutenant Nebask was hit by a piece of scrapped metal in his back, and some of the guys were looking for me and didn't know if I was in the bunker until they called my name. I said, I'm here.

The scrapped metal that hit the Lieutenant was not a large piece, yet not small, but not deadly and yet, enough to draw blood. The artillery and mortar battery dropped about twenty-five rounds in these two locations that first night.

The next morning the 2nd platoon of Alpha company, my platoon, reconned the area for bodies and the launching tubes used in the mortar and rocket attack on us the past night by the VC.

At all times praying, with my guard up, I walked through the village with my finger on the trigger and my thumb on the safety button. Just a flick from my thumb would have put my M–16 on full automatic.

I had gotten my coordination together, that I could switch my weapon to automatic and start firing as I fell to the ground. The concentration forced the synchronization of my mind and body. The tendency to be ready was always a fraction away.

We approached the hooch, but we knew that Sir Charles had left the area. We still needed to check the hooches and the bunkers. We slowly approached the hedged roll, but did not enter. We were unaware or did not know if it was booby trapped or not.

I contacted our company CP: Alpha 6, this is Alpha 2 over, this is Alpha 6 go ahead, over. We approached a hedged roll about fifty meters in front of us, we are to move fifty meters, to the south west, over. Alpha 6, said, we'll have momma bear sending a Willie Peter over; Alpha 2 over; Alpha 6, that will be in five, over. The WP rounds landed and I called Alpha 6 to have the artillery shelling stopped after the sixth round.

Then we moved into the open area. We had to spread out, not wanting to be bunched up, then we would be sitting ducks for Sir Charles. We provided cover for the point man as he went across the open field. Cover was provided for each man as we crossed the open field to the other side, before we moved into each hooch.

The demo man blew a mortar round shell that had not exploded from the last night's mortar fire at the VC. So the composition four (C-4) was placed on the mortar shell and the demo man yelled, Fire in the hole!; fire in the hole!; fire in the hole! three times. We got down to keep from being hit by the scrapped metal. We snuggled close to the ground, praying that we would not get hit by the detonated round fragments.

The round exploded. We got up and started walking through the jungle like a lion stalking his prey. Then machine gunfire erupted to the front and rear area of our platoon. The M–79 grenade launcher guy ran to the rear of the platoon. I was the RTO in the front, with the Lieutenant, and the other RTO was in the rear with the sergeant.

I called Alpha 2/6, Alpha 2/6 come in, over this is Alpha 2, over; Alpha 2/6 we found someone in the area, over; Alpha 2 roger that, we are on our way, Alpha 2, out.

This was done in case we were separated. We would still be able to maintain radio contact with one another. We found the bamboo shoots used by the VCs to launch the mortars and rockets.

They were sticking up out of the ground, we could see Diamond II about a thousand meters away and saw craters made from the mortar rounds that had been fired the last night from our mortar platoon.

My back started to give me some trouble from carrying this radio, but the Lieutenant didn't want me to stop being the radio operator. As we continued sweeping the area we saw mama-san so we stopped her and asked for her ID.

She did not understand the Lieutenant, so I asked her for her ID in Vietnamese. Then she reached into the pocket of her jacket and pulled out her ID.

When I looked at her ID, she asked me if I spoke Vietnamese. I said, Tee-tee in Vietnamese (meaning very little). According to her ID she was eighty-four years old. I told them to let the lady go, she was now responsible for her village, being the oldest person.

It must have been around noon time, so Lieutenant Nebask felt that this village area was a good place to take a break. Every man spread out to eat his C-ration and provide guard duty so Sir Charles would not walk in upon us.

I had sat down on a red-ant's nest, not aware that I had done that. They began crawling over and up the radio. Then this guy named Yates said, Joe you have red ants all over you. I immediately unfastened the radio and pulled off my shirt. Yates and Ed brushed the red ants off my back and helped me get them off of the radio.

This was one of those days that you just look up into the sky and give thanks to God, for just one more day. I had 307 days left in this country and was 58 days closer to home.

After this battle with the red ants and everything had settled down. It was time to move out. We then saddled up. I felt like an old timer, like I had been in Vietnam close to a year, because now I had been through a lot, I thought, and have by the grace of God learned how to enjoy myself no matter what the conditions.

God knew I wanted no part of Nam and very much wanted to be home. His touch allowed this transformation to take place, for it was good and I knew not what lay ahead.

It was very sad that the village people had no say in what happened to their village, family, friends, or themselves. We Americans bombed their villages, if we received gunfire, rockets, mortars, or any fire power from that village, not knowing that the VC may be holding the people in the village at gun point until they launched mortars, rockets, or took shots at us.

We would just return gunfire in that direction killing innocent people that were just farmers. These hooches were built out of bamboo structure, with rice stalks for their roof and mud elevated about a foot high for the floors, which kept the hooch dry when it rained.

As we continued our recon and the sweep of the area, we had to enter this open area once we left the hedged roll.

This was always dangerous, to be in the open. As we crossed the field, gunfire rang out. We immediately returned gunfire back at the hedger roll.

I called our CP: Alpha 6, this is Alpha 2 over, this is Alpha 6 roger, Alpha 2 over, Alpha 6 we are receiving gunfire; Alpha 2 over, Alpha 6, said gave me your grit cores, Alpha 6 over, Alpha 2 grit cores latitude, longitude, Alpha 2 over.

This is Alpha 6 roger that, over and out, Alpha 2 out. Artillery was fired into the area with the first round a WP followed by two HE rounds. We had walked into an ambush. We hit the ground to protect ourselves from the gunfire; we were unable to return gunfire; we were pinned down and needed help from the rear support units (artillery).

Our only way out was to use artillery fire to destroy the VC ambush. A few of the guys were trying to return fire. I returned gunfire, then I got on the radio to call for artillery to hit 100 meters in front of us. The artillery landed very close to us, because we were in close contact with the VC.

This is Alpha 6, Alpha 2 over, this is Alpha 6 are we on target, over, Alpha 2 roger that, Alpha 6, Alpha 2 stop firing, stop firing, no more small weapon fire, over, Alpha 6 roger that, Alpha 6, Alpha 2 out.

Alpha 6 this is Alpha 2, we are moving forward to check the area out over, Alpha 6 roger that, out. As we moved into the area that gunfire was received from and was fired upon by our artillery unit, we remained in contact with Alpha 6 to let them know what we found. Alpha 2 over, Alpha 6 roger got your message out.

Then we stopped firing our weapons and began our search for this VC that was so bold to shoot at us. As we approached the hedged roll, there was a very thin wire strung across the hedged roll; a booby trap that would have exploded if we did not use precaution in our hot pursuit.

The thin wire gave us no clue to its end so we called the demo guy from the rear of the platoon to blow this booby trap. The demo guy found the end of the wire; it was connected to an artillery shell that was dropped by the Americans sometime ago, but had not yet exploded.

The VC rigged it to blow once we trapped the wire. The demo guy set the charge with a ten-minute fuse that gave us plenty of time to be further away from the area when it blew up. We blew all booby traps or items used as part of a booby trap so they could not be used against us, at some time later on.

We made it to the area and found no one. We stayed in contact with the CP. Radio silence was not needed; Sir Charles already knew where we were. We wanted to make sure that our CP was in contact with us just in case we needed mortar or artillery support.

I looked at the map to give the CP our direction latitude and longitude in order that the mortar and artillery units would know where to place their shelling: 100 meters to the east, west, north, or south.

We then asked permission to enter the parameter from Alpha 6. The AK–47 gunfire rang out, we hit the dirt as we were walking into the front gates. No one was hit. The Lieutenant reported to the CP to see the Captain once we removed our gear.

We had a hot meal that evening and I picked up the mail for our platoon. I had received my package that my brothers wrote and told me about in September. This was November, around the 15th of the month. I opened the rest of the package because it was already halfway open when I received it.

My brothers had sent me some music and some food,

so you know that the music went on real quick. You know some of the brothers in our platoon were singing and dancing to the music and the Caucasian guys also tried to sing and dance. This was a break from the normal things after getting the music and the tape with some comedy.

As night drew closer the music went off and we prepared ourselves for the events that might occur this night. We did not get fired upon that night from the VC; maybe it was because we destroyed their bamboo rocket tubes.

The next day we remained in Diamond II to wash our faces and brush our teeth. Even though it had been two days, it seemed a lot longer than that since our last bath.

We spent the next twelve days patrolling this area outside of Diamond II. One night on patrol we sat up in a dried-out rice paddy having very little cover. If we encountered an attack, it would have been very difficult for us to defend ourselves from Sir Charles. It was just that bad, just like some of the other site locations selected by our Lieutenant.

From our platoon we dispatched a five-man alert patrol (LP) to warn us of any activity if they saw any movement in our direction. We only had 20 guys in our platoon; now we had five less and the LP patrol was about 500 meters to our front.

The night was cool as the wind blew around, and the mosquitoes were very bad and hungry. So we placed our poncho liners over our bodies as we laid on our backs, covering ourselves from the mosquitoes.

The best insect repellent for the mosquitoes in Nam was the military brand. The insect repellent Off and any other stateside insect spray that we received from home, prepared those vampire mosquitoes to feast on us. When the stateside repellent is used, it makes it easier for the mosquitoes to draw our blood.

These mosquitoes were not the American variety type

of mosquitoes; these were the B–52 type dive bombers. They were the size of the American bumble-bee. I was tired, but I guess I started getting used to not having any sleep.

As the night grew later, it was my turn to pull guard duty. We would always communicate with the LP unit, not knowing if they had heard me, by asking them to squelch twice, where they push the button on the phone set twice.

Because the LP unit was not visible, it was also a possibility that Sir Charles could have crawled up and killed the five man LP unit and started moving in our direction. I spent that watch looking as far as I possibly could; looking in the night at tree lines, the sky, small trees, and long rolls of rice stalks to be viewed, if I saw any movement by the enemy.

We must have been about 500 to 600 meters away from these hedge rolls on all sides, plus the rice paddy was so large, we could only set up, and cover three sides of the rice paddy. Did I get a feeling that something was wrong with this set up? You bet I did; that's why we placed extra claymore mines on that end of the parameter.

I then woke up another guy to pull guard duty. Guarding our location was done until the daylight hours. Around 5:30 A.M. the VC opened gunfire on us and we quickly returned gunfire in that direction. It must have been a VC trying to find out where we were or how many of us there were in the area, because he left the area quickly.

They also had village people under pressure to make them tell, what the last direction was they had seen us going in. They had more ears and eyes looking out to get us, than what we had. So we never knew what to expect at any time of the day or night.

It had been noticed that since the Wolfhounds from Alpha company arrived, the activity of rockets and mortars from the VC had been stopped. Our mortar and artillery teams kept the VC from launching their rockets and mortars against us twice a day.

The 4th platoon would fire a few shells each night in the general location where we had found the VC launching tube and have the artillery unit fire their shells 50 to 100 meters to the left or right of the mortar platoon shelling.

The second night the VC launched their rockets, and the sergeant of the mortar squad gave the grid cores to the air striker planes, they dropped small bombs on the VC location to destroy their launching area. This bombing would destroy underground tunnels, which is where Sir Charles is hiding.

Now that there has been a reduction in activity, there was a possibility for a reassignment. Crazy things like this happen all the time. Also, this guy bought some beer from this girl for two dollars. Then he noticed that the can had a big lump of solder on the side when he turned it around.

The girl was moving quickly from the front gate. He yelled to the girl, Hey come here! She then looked and ran. He told some of his buddies that bought some beer and soda not to drink them.

A couple of guys from 4th Army company were coming in from their road guard post saw the girl running and heard the GI yelling, Grab the girl!, which they did and returned her to the guy that was yelling.

He then punched her in the face. The soldier then opened the can of beer and told the girl to drink it. She said, I don't drink beer, so the GI took a piece of cloth, using it as a strainer. Then he poured the beer onto the cloth to strain it.

After the beer had passed through the cloth, and the foam went down, there it was, small crystal glass ground fine enough that it would cause internal bleeding in the stomach and intestine area. Unknown to the rest of the soldiers in Diamond II, one GI had taken a couple of drinks of his soda and had run to the medic, because he had a piece of glass in his mouth.

The CP had called for a chopper to medic-vac the soldier to a hospital for special care in the Cu-Chi area. The girl was also taken in for questioning, and would be treated as a VC prisoner of war.

We had always been told that the VC would have the children come to our camp to look and report on our artillery, mortar, radio control, and medical tent location. The Viet Cong played the game to win and everything goes; no favors. The other children and lady that were with the girl went in for interrogation. They were taken by another chopper to Cu-Chi too.

It was then told to us that no one would purchase any drinks of any kind from any Vietnamese ladies or children. If anyone made a purchase, you could be charged, and be court martialed. The Captain told us that headquarters would supply all beer and soda to the field units with a restriction of two beers per person, per day. That was great, so Ed turned to me and said, Joe, I got your beer, right? I said, Yes man, you have my beer. Ed, just don't get drunk and not be able to pull guard duty, I said.

After the beer and soda event many of the Caucasian soldiers became upset at the people in the village. We were on many eagle flights to different places to reduce the VC activities up north or in the southern area locations.

There was heavy activity in this next location that we had to eagle flight to. The choppers had machine guns mounted on each side. This was a hot LZ. I've been in one before, but each always appears different, when you don't want to go into a battle. You never knew what was going to happen to you or anyone else during a fire fight.

After the bridge duty we flew or walked to wherever

there was activity from our location. This time it was not the walk on the rice paddy dice, but more like the jungle, because of the thick tree lines and brushes.

We received some shots from the tree line. Ed fired an M–60 machine gun and Yates dropped a Highly Explosive (HE) round from his M–79 grenade launcher, along with the rest of the platoon firing their M–16 weapons. I think the VC was caught off guard by our returning the gunfire so quickly. He stopped shooting and so did we. As he ran, we ran after him, but all that was left was the VC sandals. He "dee-dee-mow" so quickly, he had to kick off those sandals, because they were slowing him down. I believe we hit him with our return fire power even if there wasn't any blood. We believe that he went into the village.

As we went through the village, some soldiers pushed things over. I had mixed emotions. I felt that they had everything to lose by that type of action. This was only done because of the beer and soda event. The fact was they could do it and nothing would be said to them about it. We had the people in the village move together in a bunch and searched the rest of the village.

We found nothing. Then on our way out of the area, we saw where the VC had left his sandals, so we went to the right and not to the left. The VCs had set a time-explosive device that went off on the left side. We would have sustained injuries if we went to the left, on our way out of the village.

We continued communicating with our CP, but no activity was reported. We popped purple smoke when the choppers were on their way back to pick us up, so the choppers would know where to land to pick us up. The choppers landed, we got on board, and they flew us back to Diamond II. We had no losses on this day and felt cheated about what happened to the VC that left his sandals.

There were still a few other things that needed to be done outside of Diamond II, so the 2nd platoon went out on road patrol the next day and remained there all day. We had to guard the road but it had to be swept for mines before we set up our watch station. The village people then got up and tended to their rice fields and the harvesting of the rice.

There was this one guy in our platoon who could draw pretty good. He drew a picture of momma-san beating the rice against the basket. She switched the rice stalks that were tied together from the right side then the left, turning the stalks each time she raised it off her shoulder. The picture was nice and the soldier gave the drawing to the lady as a gift.

Nearby, there lived a wealthy man who had rice fields, many water buffaloes, many chickens, and pigs, and lived in a brick house. He invited Lieutenant Nebask, myself, Ed, Miller, and the guy that drew the picture into his home. He told us about the activity of the VC around his home and the things that they had taken so they could keep fighting.

But he said that he was tired and broke, because he had lost most of his rice harvest and animals to the VC, but was thankful that his two daughters had not been harmed by the VC yet.

His daughters worked in the fields to harvest the rice now, because the VC had taken the men to fight, that he had hired to do this type of farm work. We then thanked him for letting us into his home and we returned to our guard post on the road.

We had our C-rations for lunch and tried to relax while on guard duty, before it was time for us to return to Diamond II for the evening. It was about 1:00 P.M. then and we would be saddling up to return to Diamond II about 4:30 P.M.

We spent much of our time talking about home. Then Lieutenant Nebask decided that he wanted to be one of the guys, so he started talking about his family and girlfriend. He and his girlfriend were engaged to be married when he returned home from Vietnam. He said some funny things about himself and how he acted the first day in the field. He told us that he was sorry for his behavior. We all said, Man we understood how you felt; we have all been there, too.

As the time approached for us to return to Diamond II for the night, we received a radio message that told us we needed to remain in our location. The Captain said, It has been reported there is heavy VC movement in this direction, so the Captain ordered us to remain at our post.

Lieutenant Nebask, a six-foot two-inch, 250-pound man, began to get uptight and said, to the Captain, Sir, we do not have enough men to hold off a battalion, nor do we have enough ammo to last us more than half an hour in a heated fire fight. The Captain said, these orders are from battalion headquarters, Alpha 2. I gave you the orders to be carried out, Alpha 6. Over and out.

The Lieutenant was pink, pale, and scared, there was thirty-five American soldiers about two miles away from Diamond II ready to do battle with two battalions or 2000 VC. This reminded me of the American Indian War, at the "Little Big Horn," between "Sitting Bull" and "Custer."

I did not like these odds, so what I suggested was that we place our claymore mines around our parameter, about fifty feet in front of us, and set out trap flares about fifteen feet in front of the claymores.

We had around thirty-five claymore mines and one-hundred grenades, and each man had about twenty-five magazines with twenty rounds in each magazine or 17,500 rounds. Ya, this sounds like a lot of fire power, but not close enough for 1000–2000 VC. They would have, in rounds, well over one million, plus mortars and RPG rocket rounds.

I knew the U.S. wanted to reduce their population, but one would think that it would have been better to have these thirty-five men on the bunker line inside Diamond II to help defend this camp. Instead of making these thirty-five men sacrifice their lives so that the camp is warned by radio or gunfire that the VC are on their way to Diamond II.

That night the movement shifted and the VC approached Diamond II from the opposite direction. The guys pulling guard duty on the bunker line spotted movement just before the trapped flare went off. The mortar platoon, artillery battery and the bunker line on the east side of Diamond II opened gunfire on the VC.

The Lieutenant and I listened to the radio and the Captain called us to tell us to be prepared because they had Sir Charles on the run and he was moving in our direction. We continued listening to the gunfire tee, tee, boom, boom, bams as the M–16 gunfire, mortar rounds, and artillery rounds landed. It was frightening; the exchanges lasted for about thirty minutes and then started to taper off.

Through the star-light-scope we looked around to see if Sir Charles was heading our way. I was on the right side of the road and the first squad of 2nd platoon was in the hedged roll. They signaled that they heard movement coming our way. We waited for about five minutes, then first squad opened fire. Bullets were flying everywhere, claymores exploded, grenades exploded. This lasted for about 40 seconds, then stopped.

The Captain called us and asked, Is everyone okay? I said, We are checking; Sir Charles did come this way, but we don't know if anyone is injured. The Captain wanted us to keep in contact with him until things had stopped altogether.

After calling first squad to find out what happened, they said, Sir Charles was coming and they hit some of the VC and didn't know if the bodies were pulled off by the other VC or not. We then informed the Captain and he advised us to remain in our position and recon the area on our way back in to Diamond II around 7:00 A.M. the next morning. We, "roger that message from the Captain and out."

Once it was daylight we saddled up removing our claymore mines, and trap flares; then we moved out slowly in that direction. First squad of our platoon had exchanged gunfire with the VC.

There was blood on the ground, but no bodies. We reconned and swept the area for more blood and bodies, but did not see any, so we assumed that those that were wounded, must have been picked up and carried off by the other able VCs.

We finally made it back to Diamond II and discovered that two of the bunkers that 2nd platoon normally guarded was overrun by Sir Charles and they had killed three American soldiers and two were wounded.

The mortar unit had to drop mortar rounds in that area because Sir Charles invaded the parameter. There were six VC killed at that bunker location.

God looked upon our platoon that night. If Sir Charles got in Diamond II parameter, with their two rolls of razor-sharp barbed wire three rolls high, they would have slaughtered us. We just had claymores and trap flares, and many prayers.

After we had settled in and the Lieutenants from the four platoons met with the Captain, the Lieutenants reported to us that, "The Captain told us that Alpha company would be heading for the Cambodian border in a few days by eagle flight once we received the rest of the information."

There have been meetings before between the Captain and the Lieutenants, but there was something different in the tone of the Lieutenant's voice about the Cambodian border. I asked what was, and where was the border. One guy from 4th Army company said, They were on the border in September and Sir Charles kicked the stuff out of them they___don't play on the border.

Everyone knew, based on information received from this guy in our battalion, that the Cambodian border was no place to be. The local VC we had been fighting were chumps compared to those VC on the border.

So everyone ate breakfast and afterwards began writing letters to friends and family, not knowing if this would be the last letter their families would receive from them. Later that day we had mail call and I received letters from my family; Warren, Bob, Bill, Ida, Jannie, Pauline, Mozzella, my step-mother, Phyllis, and Carolyn.

I was very glad to hear from everyone, but as I read the letters from my family, Bob, Bill, and Warren told me of a package that they had sent me, with a tape recorder in it, which they had sent around the twentieth of September. They didn't know that I had already received the package, and I had told them thank you in the last letter I had written to them. I guess they had not received my letter yet. I guess it really takes six to eight weeks to send and receive mail.

But, they said that everyone was doing just fine, but missed me a whole lot, wishing that I was home. They took my very thoughts as I was getting prepared to go on the border. I would have been home in a half of a heart beat, if I could.

The letter I received from Phyllis said that she missed me and wished that I was home and that these two months seemed like years and said, With love see you soon! Carolyn was a Sagittarius and was very explosive in her letter, telling me what not to do with any of those girls there. She also sang in our group called the "Golden Bells Singers," with my brother Warren, two sisters Mozzella and Pauline and myself.

My step-mother wanted me to date Carolyn, but I told my step-mother that she was not my size and that I didn't like her enough to date. But my step-mother and her daughter Mozzella told Carolyn that I liked her, so when we had to rehearse over at our house my step-mother would put Carolyn and me together. At first I said, Okay, then I said, No I wanted to date Renee. I liked her more than I did Carolyn.

But my step-mother said she would see to it that I started dating Carolyn and that was that. I was in tenth grade then and Christmas was near, but I had a part-time job working at a restaurant as a junior chief.

My step-mother told me to buy Carolyn a Christmas gift, but I said to my step-mother that I would buy her a gift as a member of the group, but not as my girlfriend. My step-mother told me that I was going to buy Carolyn a good gift like a watch. Due to other circumstances, I bought the watch for Carolyn.

So in this letter I received from Carolyn, she told me when I got home we were going to get married and that was that. I wrote her back and told her that she better find someone else and not to write and tell me not to see any of these Vietnamese ladies.

It was nice receiving the letters from everyone, even the letter from Carolyn. I had life and death looking me right in my face and I did not like it. For her to tell me what not to do, I guess the timing was all wrong. She is a nice person and needed someone better than I. My life is___I have a battle to deal with.

Finally the orders came the next day. We were to leave Diamond II on November 19, 1968, for the Cambodian border. The Captain told the four Lieutenants to inform their platoons to field scrap their weapons and magazines, so that they were clean for this mission. Get plenty of ammo and take extra claymore mines, grenades, socks, and the rest of our field gear.

The package I received from home and any other items were sent into battalion headquarters in Cu-Chi to the supply room with our names on these items.

I thought to myself, it must be really bad there, that's for sure. Then Ed said, I don't want this M–16 gun any longer; I'll be a machine gunner now. This Caucasian guy gladly gave up the machine gun and took Ed's M–16. He said, he was tired of carrying this heavy weapon, but Ed also asked for a .45-caliber hand gun just in case the M–60 jammed, from too many rounds of ammo fire through the weapon.

IX

The Wolfhounds Meet the Regular V.C. Army (NVA)

It was about 7:00 A.M. that morning of November 19, 1968. It was quiet. We had a hot breakfast with hash browns, eggs scrambled or any way you wanted them, orange juice, milk, toast, jelly, and seconds if you wanted it. I didn't know if this was our last meal or just our last hot meal. Even the birds sang one song. What was with this day, that was so different from what was normal?

It was like everything or everybody knew that this was the day for us to go to the border and everything had some idea of what could possibly happen, while we were there. So did we, and the feeling wasn't good at all.

You could hear the choppers coming, far off, for us, to eagle flight us near the Cambodian border. Normally the Hornet chopper pilots flew us to many landing zones (hot or cold) and this was a big eagle flight; the first for the entered company.

Cambodia was considered to be a neutral country, but the U.S. allowed troops from China and Japan to enter in this war, because it would create diplomatic problems later on if they could not enter this war. Well, as we boarded the choppers, the units left to guard Diamond II, and wished us well on this most dangerous mission.

Just one month ago, Charlie company, who was part of our battalion, went to the border. The regular VC army (NVA) overran their position, leaving them with major loss.

Charlie company went from 125 men down to fifty men, and some who sustained wounds, were able to walk away.

The only reason the entire company was not destroyed one of the guys from Charlie company said, was that he thinks the VC had ran out of ammo and did not know if Charlie company had too.

Even though the VC made it in the parameter and blew up the CP, many of the VC were killed by the blast as well, and from M–16 gunfire from the U.S. (Charlie company Wolfhounds) troops. This was the company that our friend Madlock was assigned to.

The gun ship helicopter arrived just in time to further beat the VC back off of Charlie company. We sent the VC back over the border, dragging as many of their dead VC bodies back with them as possible. The guy from Charlie company said, based on the type of attack we were under, it must have been two battalions of VC.

I told this guy, Thank you for drawing and painting this picture for us, because we really needed to know all of this. Now my blood pressure is up and a lump has lodged in my throat. But we thanked him and prepared ourselves for that day's eagle flight.

The choppers landed on the road and Alpha company went out of the gate to climb on board. As each chopper lifted, the runner of the chopper appeared to be a foot off the ground as we began our flight. Then we flew as high as the tree tops, flying at great speed; then we rose just enough to look down upon the trees and the villages. Finally we were at our maximum height for this flight.

We were escorted by gun ships to our left and right flank with a loch helicopter as a spotter chopper for the gun ships flew far ahead of the chopper convoy. We flew for about twenty minutes, which placed us about two or three clicks from the Cambodian border.

Again the gun ships prepped the area as the choppers came in for landing and as quickly as we had jumped off the choppers, they flew away. As we moved out, you could hear the fading away of the chopping sound, the sound of the helicopter propeller grew soft as the distance became greater. As we spread ourselves out, we took cover just in case we had landed in a hot LZ, and were not aware that we had.

Then the Captain gave each Lieutenant their area to sweep and recon in order that all four platoons would meet at a location by 2:00 P.M. that afternoon.

Then 2nd platoon took off and we were heading southwest, sweeping around the canal area or swamplike location. It was hot that day, but the good thing was that we did not walk too far, just one and a half clicks (almost two miles).

As we looked along this hedged roll there was a mortar round that never exploded, because once it hit the mud it just sank. This had happened a great deal, due to the climate. It rained about seven to eight times a day; the ground does stay wet and keeps artillery and mortar rounds from exploding unless the shell hits a hard surface.

Our demo man set an explosive charge for five minutes, which blew the mortar round after we had left the area. The sky was a pretty blue color and the clouds were puffy and white. There was a little breeze that helped keep us a little cooler than normal, because the sun made things very hot.

Then we spotted a Russian-made tank across the Cambodian border, but I don't know if they had seen us because we were pretty well covered by the hedged roll as we patrolled this area. Then we saw a loch helicopter flying overhead. The tank then moved from off the hillside. The tank may have taken a position off the hillside to be able to shoot down the loch helicopter or to hide itself.

Then there was artillery fire, our rear support unit firing Willie Peter rounds to mark their location that would provide backup support for us if we were under attack. Then the gun ship from Cam-Ron-Bay fired their marker round again to provide rear support for us.

Because they were test marker rounds, the loch helicopter made sure that the artillery unit and gun ship from Cam-Ron-Bay did not fire their rounds into Cambodia. All rounds, no matter what, had to land on Vietnam soil.

The 2nd and 3rd platoon had completed their recon sweep and was heading for the location that had been selected by the Captain. It was secure by 1st and 4th platoon. We arrived to this location about 1:00 P.M. Shortly thereafter, a shounook helicopter arrived with additional supplies: M–16 and M–60 ammo, M–79 launcher ammo, laws rockets, mortar rounds, sand bags, medical supplies, shelves, and C-rations.

I guess from the looks of things this was going to be a big battle if there was one at all. After everything was distributed to all the squads, we tried to dig up this ground, in this old dried-out rice field, which had not been used for a long time. This soil was like a rock. However, we were able to dig down only eight to nine inches. When fox holes, for fighting, are as deep as five feet, boy I think we are in trouble.

We also received two fifty-caliber machine guns, which went to the 2nd and 3rd platoon, because the 2nd platoon was located on the north east corner of the parameter and the 3rd was located on the southwest corner of the parameter. This would give 2nd platoon a field of fire from north and east and 3rd south and west. These were big shells that would be fired from the fifty-caliber machine guns and anti-aircraft and anti-tank weapon.

Since Ed Dow was our machine gunner, he received this anti-aircraft and anti-tank weapon. The shells or rounds were about six inches long. Ed began cleaning this big machine gun, pouring LSA oil upon and into the barrel and trigger housing for possible action later this day.

Ed found this spot in the hedged roll. It looked like a natural machine gun nest created by nature for Ed to set his M–60 and fifty-caliber machine gun side-by-side, directed at the Cambodian border.

My nine-inch deep fox hole that was four feet long and a sleeping area that was nine inches in depth and six feet long was about fifty feet away from Ed's machine gun nest.

The entire company spent the remainder of that day setting up and preparing for a battle that we had no idea would be real to life. "What happens, you know, would have been fine for television, perfect action for about three hours!"

We ate our C-rations for lunch and supper and the Captain made his rounds to each of our so-called fox holes and asked if we were ready and that, we better pray, this was going to be a big one.

Everyone had placed claymore mines about twenty feet in front of their fox holes along with trip flares that were ten feet in front of the claymore mines. It had been decided that there were going to be two LP patrols sent out (suicide mission squads) as early warning units to spot VC movement and report it to the main parameter to get ready for action once the VC were spotted.

The 2nd and 3rd platoon had to supply a squad to do this mission, sending five men from each squad. It must have been about 5:00 P.M., when we spotted the VC crossing the Cambodian border walking into Vietnam. We said, These VC don't have on any pajamas, they're fully geared up, just like us.

The Captain came over to Ed's machine gun nest, with his binoculars to see if he could get a closer look at these guys walking from Cambodia into Nam. They were about one or two miles away in a open field on the soil of Vietnam.

They were also looking at us, with their binoculars. These guys were very bold and they sent a chill down our spines. We wondered if they were going to keep going or attack us later that night. Around 7:00 P.M. two PCs (personnel carriers) arrived from an armor unit four miles from our location.

The Captain must have called headquarters and told them about the VCs walking over the border; then, headquarters contacted the armor unit to have the PCs dispatched to our company location.

Well we waited and talked, but our conversation was not about death. It was about the good times we had had, while each of us were at home, both Caucasians and African Americans.

Everyone knew that bullets did not discriminate, and then it was said, We are Wolfhounds. The Captain walked around again as the LP units had saddled up to go to their early warning location areas.

It was 9:00 P.M., and all was well. The moon was out that night. That was strange, I said to myself. You normally do not see the moon until the end of the month and the first five days in the next month.

Ed and his two partners went over to the machine gun nest to watch for Sir Charles, as did the rest of 2nd platoon and the whole company.

As the night moved into the early morning, where everyone had just about pulled their guard duty, the reports from the LP patrols said things were quiet.

Then it happened, around 3:30 A.M. that morning of

November 20, 1968. The first round of the gun battle was shot at both LP patrols. Unbeknownst to us, the VC wounded everyone on 2nd platoons LP and the VC told them that they would be back after they overran the main parameter.

The VC had killed three guys in the 3rd platoon LP and wounded the other two guys and told them the same thing: that they would return for them after they had overtaken the main parameter.

Everyone in the parameter was ready from hearing the gun shots fired from each LP patrol and the radio call they made, to us, for help as they identified their wounded and dead.

They said, they're coming for you! they're coming for you! Sir Charles sent off an RPG rocket round that landed in front of one, of the PC's carriers, killing one guy and wounding two others.

The VC then opened fire on Ed's and my fox hole area. Ed was shot in the hand and the assistant machine gunner was shot in the chest. The other guy got up and ran, yelling, "We're being overrun! We're being overrun!"

As the bullets went over my head, as I laid there, I said, "Doo Doo Doo Doo," as I crawled from my sleeping area into the fox hole. I took two grenades; as the guys in my fox hole continued firing their weapons, and I threw the grenades out in front of our fox hole, because the gunfire was coming close to our area.

It was heavy, but was reduced from the grenades I had thrown. I was caught up in this gun battle, without knowing what if or why I did what I did. Then I got up and ran over to Ed. He had wrapped his hand and was still firing the M–60 machine gun. Ed said that the M–50 caliber machine gun jammed after the first burst of about fifty rounds.

I yelled, Medic! medic! medic!, but he was very busy with the other guys so I took my bandage off my helmet and placed the inside plastic part over the chest area of the wounded guy, and put the remaining bandage on as tightly as possible around the chest area. The assistant machine gunner had a sucking chest wound. The bleeding and the air needed to be stopped from going into the chest.

Ed was firing his M–60 machine gun, while I took care of this guy then that gun jammed (M– 60), so Ed took the M–16 that was lying next to the guy that was wounded. We started firing our M–16s, returning gunfire to the VC.

For a moment I was thinking, vacant villages, cemetery, this was the only battle that I had been in, 150 man company against a 1000-VC battalion. I had reacted to the situation with a so-called clear mind. But it was clear and I wasn't sure about what was going on at all. Ed and I just put the magazines in and replaced them when they were empty. I used my M–16; ammo magazines like water running out of a fountain, that's how fast I was firing my weapon.

The smell of gun powder, an unearthly odor, like burned leaves and grass with flesh blended together, gives you the feeling that death is near. I thought to myself this was the end of my dreams. Ed had a piece of scrapped metal in his stomach but it was close to the surface as he pulled it from his stomach and continued firing.

Sir Charles had a method to his madness of wounding the LP patrol only to return to where they are after they overrun the main parameter to kill all that are not dead. I wiped my face in order to see clearly any moving objects, to blow them away. It was them or us and right now we had this parameter and they got to come and get it.

I told Ed to pour the LSA oil on the M–60 machine gun barrel. That gun had fired so many rounds that the barrel was white hot and was bent from the heat to the right, slightly. The LSA oil would cool the M–60 machine gun enough so that Ed would be able to begin firing it again.

Sir Charles then stopped firing and told us to surrender our weapons because we were surrounded by two battalions of VCs and we would not make it out alive, if we did not surrender.

Just then an RPG rocket landed next to the CP, wounding two other guys. We were losing men one way or another, by death or being seriously wounded, putting us out of action. The CP called for rear support, but the artillery unit could not fire their shells because it would wipe out our company if they dropped the shells that close to the parameter.

The Captain, you could hear him, yelling on the horn, as he cursed___,we are being overrun, just fire___the shells, but the artillery unit would not provide us with the support needed to turn this losing battle around. God knew what it took and the soldiers that were able kept defending their area from the VC.

The Captain yelled as he stayed on the horn: There is no need to talk in code!! The VC are overrunning our position! We need your support now!! He was truly___cursing (every word he could use).

Neither the artillery unit from Cu-Chi nor Cam-Ron-Bay would provide backup, but the shark gunners' gun ships were beautiful. These special helicopters, shaped like a jet plane, loaded with rockets, grenades, machine guns, and mortar rounds, had to refuel, but stopped by about 5:00 A.M., as the clouds started rolling in.

You could smell the gun powder from everything that had exploded. Then we heard the chopping sound of the gun ship helicopter. We marked our location with purple smoke, in order that the gunners would not mistake us and shoot inside of our parameter, but for them to fire their rounds in front of us where the VC were.

We continued battling with Sir Charles, but the gun ship backed the VC up and they ran back across the border, taking what dead they could with them.

This was an experience with bullets flying overhead seen by the red tracers every tenth round. I was unable to move because the instant burst of bullets zinged across my body. I laid still until there was a break in the VC's shooting so I would be able to move.

I then turned away to return gunfire back at the VC. This was unreal and I did not know fear at this time, but only life and what I thought it meant to me. We shot aerial flares, ground flares, that aluminized the sky and the night had turned bright as day from that explosion.

It was brighter than on the 4th of July, guys yelling for the Medic! medic! medic! because of being hit from bullets, or RPG rounds scrapped, melted, crying for help, and yet not sure if you could make over to them alive if you tried.

We had to be careful firing our weapons, because our LP was 200 feet to the left of our fox hole. We had to reduce our field of fire, because the LP had called to tell us that they were hit and needed a medic quickly.

The 2nd platoon LP was on a little piece of land that would be covered as the tide rolled in with the water. They said, The water is rising and we need help with the seriously wounded. We blew the claymore mines because Sir Charles was twenty feet in front of us and all around us you could hear, boom! boom! boom! boom!, ta-ta-ta-ta-ta.

Sir Charles knew how to use psychological games on you, because he told us to surrender once again, that they had us outnumbered ten to one. There were too many bullets flying everywhere. Ed's M–60 jammed again, then Sir Charles charged Ed. He pulled his .45 pistol and fired it with fear. He killed two VC. I ran back to his location to assist him. This time the Wolfhounds wanted to be out of there, but could not give up, because of life itself.

We had tasted our blood and to die would have been okay if it was meant to be. But we just could not give up; we kept the battle going from these men that were still fighting from within and without of this battle against the VC.

Our company was already small in size, no more than a hundred-and-five men, and we had already suffered losses that reduced the size down to seventy-five men. I thank God, for his protection, this night, God could have, but he did not, leave us without support. Because I know I was and Ed was, and the other guys had been praying that it was possible for the gun ships to return just in time.

After about one hour the gunfiring stopped from the gun ship and the VC. This battle went from 3:30 to 6:00 A.M.: gunfire, mortar rounds, rockets, and grenades exploding for nearly three hours.

The gun ships had to return to Cu-Chi. Their fuel had begun running low and they were out of ammo. Also, the fog had become very heavy, which made it more difficult for the gun ships to see.

So they left us in our position. Each platoon checked for casualties for medical evaluation. A couple of guys went out to help our wounded on the LP.

Then the Captain wanted each platoon to saddle up and search for the VC, dead or alive. It was around 7:00 A.M. when we were leaving the parameter to get a body count of the enemy.

So I picked up my radio, but the antenna had been damaged by bullets. The radio was laying on the ground where I was sleeping. My poncho liner was also damaged by bullets. I received a chill from my head to the bottom of my feet, as I thanked God for giving me swiftness in moving out of that sleeping area.

I then grabbed the radio, my M–16, and ammo to go on this search for VC bodies. We all were still afraid to go out of the parameter, because we didn't know if Sir Charles was laying low, waiting for us to come out to check for a body count.

Sir Charles has also been known to pull the grenade pin, as he is dying and allow his body to rest upon the handle of the grenade to explode seconds after you turn the dead body over.

We had to be careful. Lieutenant Nebask spotted movement in the brushes as we walked out of our parameter. He turned to shoot the VC, but his gun jammed. I immediately switched my M–16 to automatic. I was afraid, I was upset at the Lieutenant for not having taken better care of his weapon; otherwise, it would not have jammed on him.

I was really upset with myself. This was the first time that I had seen myself kill. Yes, during this entire battle I may have killed many VCs. I may have wounded some VCs, in other small encounters before now.

In just seconds, I had taken a life and others had seen me do this. I was hurt, because I took a life. Not because it was the enemy trying to take my life, no, but me, "thou shalt not kill."

Even though I had my weapon on fully automatic, I fired three quick rounds, and I watched each round hit the VC's body, moving his body backwards as the rounds hit him in his chest.

The Lieutenant yelled, Stop! stop! stop! I then smelled the gunpowder from my M–16 and as I removed my finger and placed my weapon on safety, I became numb to what I had done.

It wasn't right, I had to live with this the rest of my life even though I asked God forgiveness. We moved away from that area to continue our sweep in search of dead or alive VC bodies.

Then there was gunfire to our right, but no one was hit. We returned gunfire, 3rd platoon was also next to the area returning gunfire to that same location, where we, 2nd platoon, had started firing at the VC.

Then the VC lifted up a white handkerchief on a stick. We then stopped shooting and told the VC to stand up. Then 3rd platoon escorted the VC to our parameter where the Captain was located, where arrangements were made to take the VC back to Cu-Chi for interrogation.

The 2nd platoon continued looking for bodies to report back to the Captain. We had seen trails of blood in the tall brush where they had been pushed down from the bodies of the VC that had been dragged off by the able VC soldiers back across the Cambodian border.

We then received news of G.I. soldiers that were killed during this heavy battle. These two guys had seen Sir Charles early that night around 2:00 A.M., but were too high from smoking pot, which made them unable to warn us. We could have reduced the attack, had we received that information.

They were part of the armor unit, which was part of those that joined our company later that evening, before it became dark.

So these guys were laughing at Sir Charles as he moved into position to engage in their attack against us. The RPG round that we heard, had landed next to the PC carrier, killing both men. That round triggered the battle. This information came from a guy in the armor unit.

The 2nd platoon made it to 3rd platoon LP patrol location and we discovered two other soldiers that caught Sir Charles off guard during this battle. They had, also been killed.

I had to call and give their names in code over the radio, so that Sir Charles would not (if they were on our radio frequency) be able to understand who they were in order that they would not find the person's address, and be able to locate and send a letter to that dead GI's family that may cause some problems.

I also gave the names of the five men that were seriously wounded. The other wounded, were taken care of by the medics in each company.

As the morning moved on, it was 10:00 A.M., someone said that we were going to move, but remain on the border, just at a different location. The Captain was informed that there was heavy activity from the VC crossing the Cambodian border and they wanted Alpha company to remain in this area.

So we gathered up our ammo, claymore mines, trip flares, weapons, C-rations, and every man that remained who was able to fire his weapon, and we moved back two clicks (two miles) and started setting up our defense. The Captain CP asked the rear support supply unit in Cu-Chi to send us some barbed wire.

This would help in slowing the VC down and it would reduce the possibility of being overrun by the VC. We moved slowly, because of our being fatigued from the battle and some of the wounded that were not seriously injured, that remained with us. God knows we needed every man we could possibly have for the next VC battle and it wasn't going to be nice.

After about three hours of sweeping the area for more VC bodies, leaving from the close area of the border where we had set up the night before, we spotted a location for our defenses an area less than two clicks away.

The area was shaped like a square much like the last location, but the hedger roll there was much thicker. That also meant more danger for us. You, see, the RPG rounds that are fired from the VCs just needed to hit the hedger roll and have scrapped metal flying all over, wounding us, or killing us with every round that's fired.

This hedger roll also offered us camouflaged cover from the VCs. If we moved around in the parameter, it made it impossible to be noticed.

There was a long hedger roll line leading into the parameter hedger roll that connected into the location we had selected, which was very dangerous. Everyone thought that it stated in the "Geneva Convention," signed during World War II, that no one should use booby traps.

Somehow, the VC did not attend this meeting or read this document and we decided to turn the tables in our favor. Our first location, that we left, the demo man placed composition four (C-4) charges and barbed wire booby traps, in the hedged roll.

We also placed Willie Peter (WP) rounds in the new location in the long hedger roll that was connected to the rest of the parameter. We had to follow these stupid rules (The Geneva Convention) but the VC didn't. The United States lost many men due to Sir Charle's booby traps.

As a Wolfhound, Sir Charles had placed a thousand dollar bounty on each of our heads and he almost collected it that time, in our first border battle. Thank God for the gun ships. Before it was night we boobied everything that would be a way of entry for Sir Charles to launch his attack.

There was a crematory on the right side of the parameter, we ran trap flares, and set up booby traps in the crematory. We cut down the elephant grass to have a clear field of fire; that allowed us to have 180 degrees field of fire we needed.

Trees, headstones big and small, rice dices, tall grass in between locations, about 200 feet out we had booby trapped that area. We gave ourselves an edge, that we had not had in the first battle.

It no longer mattered if Sir Charles had a battalion or two or three; no one would remember. If Sir Charles tried to overrun us this time, everything would be blown at once.

It was so bad, the guys that had four and eight weeks left in the country had to be air lifted by helicopter to our new location, because of our loss of men from the first battle. These guys that were short, in time, were now more afraid than they ever had been before.

Because at this point in your tour of duty your mind is on home, not a war, but home, sweet home! They were upset, and wanted more than anything else to go home, they were too close to home, they tasted home, they smelled home, and would kill anything around them that would keep them from going home!

You had to be here to understand what men go through in a war, but especially Vietnam. The best trained soldier the U.S. has ever had, the worst war the U.S. has ever been in. NO FRONT LINE!! You fought and died or lived where you set up camp that day or night.

That day, Stucky, Andy, Yates, Rick, Lemon, Robert, and Dave were brought to our new location, so we could defend it, under battle. It was two days before Thanksgiving, November 1968, and there had not been any attack by the VCs.

Pulling guard duty was even more of a uneasy feeling. The longer you stayed up, the more your eyes started giving you visions of things not there. So you stretch your eyes to make sure that what you saw, you really saw.

You did not want to alarm the rest of the company falsely. We had increased the number of machine guns for all platoons; the M–60 would be able to return more rounds faster than the M–16.

We also received a couple of nineties (M–90) bazookas, with bee-hive rounds. Later that night Lieutenant Nebask asked Meatball and me to man the fox hole on the east side of the parameter. When we arrived at the fox hole, I noticed that there was tall grass right in front of the fox hole.

I was afraid and upset that this was not cleared. Sir Charles could have taken this area and walked in on us, overrunning the parameter, killing everyone.

This grass was five feet tall. No way was I going to let this grass remain so that Meatball and I would not be able to see the VCs crawling through this grass. My blood pressure, 500, sweat, tears, and madness, we are going to die, if we do not cut this grass down.

So Meatball and I told the guys on each side of our fox holes not to shoot us, because we needed to cut the grass down to have a field of fire. Then Meatball and I cut the grass down in order that each fox hole on either side of us could see our field of fire, and increased everyone else's field of fire on that side of the parameter.

We then placed our claymore mines and some trip flares as quickly as we possibly could, trying to restrict our movement as much as possible. We had tied claymore mines to the trees and then noticed another heavy grass area; it was a gap about twenty feet wide. My skin began to crawl, but I just prayed and asked the Lord to help us make it through this night.

If we were not attacked that night, the next morning, if no one else would help me, I would clear the area myself. I told the guys in each fox hole to stay awake and be careful, this is not television, there is no replay. When Sir Charles comes, you only receive one change get it right don't blow it by falling asleep.

Even though the night was dark, and knowing that we could be under attack any minute, it was also shocking to have a crematory 200 feet in front of you. Meatball and I rotated guard duty and the person not on guard could only rest his body, but his mind was very active, because of where we were and the possibility of something happening as it had two days ago. Today was Wednesday, November 27, 1968. It was a cool night; we were staring at the stars, and tuned into the events of the border. I laid on my back as Meatball whispered to me about what we should do if we come under attack.

I told him first to pray and then be cool, when he starts firing his M-16. Just don't shoot your weapon, make sure you're shooting at a VC, when you start shooting.

It must have been about 4:00 A.M., that morning, when Sir Charles attacked our parameter, on the west, north, and south sides. God heard my prayers, because the east side, our side, where Meatball and I were, the Lord kept the VC away.

You could hear the boom! boom! boom! and ta-ta-ta-ta-ta, as bullets zinged through the parameter flying over our heads. I could hear the M-60, M-90, M-16, M-79 fired and grenades exploding. Then for about two seconds everything stopped.

Then there were RPG rounds launched. One hit the back of a fox hole, where there were short times (Stucky and Andy), killing both of them. Yates was further down in the fox hole and was able to detonate the claymore mines and WP rounds that exploded in the long hedged roll that was connected to the square parameter hedged roll.

But during this launching of their RPG rounds by the VC, the VC managed to overrun that fox hole. Yates had gotten out of the fox hole, after he had detonated both booby traps and ran to a tree that was seventy-five feet behind their fox hole, for cover.

As the VC had detected Yates's, movement to the tree,

they started firing their AK-47 automatic weapon at him. Yates had an M–79 grenade launcher and only had two bee-hive rounds and six HE rounds (highly-explosive).

He fired the bee-hive round, killing two VC that were ten feet away; then he fired the other bee-hive round, killing three more VC that were closer to their fox hole. Then Yates yelled, Out! and said that his fox hole was over-run and there are VC in our parameter.

Three other VC ran down in the direction of our company CP, where the Captain, First Sergeant, and the main radio controls were located. The 2nd platoon notified the CP of the VCs in the parameter and told the Captain that they were moving in his direction.

The VC reached the CP tent; they were armed with plastic explosive (Saco Charges), but the CP team saw the VC coming, opened fire on one VC, and killed him. The other VC threw his plastic explosive and ran off before it exploded.

The 3rd platoon shot and killed that VC and the 1st and 2nd platoon killed the other VC inside the parameter. The plastic explosive thrown by the other VC threw scrapped metal everywhere, which killed one of the CP radio operators and wounded two other soldiers.

Then the Captain got on the horn (radio) and called for rear support from the artillery unit, big guns, in Cam-Ron-Bay. They started firing their guns. You could hear those artillery shells whistle through the air, landing a hundred feet in front of our parameter.

Scrapped metal zinged through the air, still red hot. This jagged piece of metal was ready to hit something or someone, cutting, boring into, whatever it hit. Lieutenant Nebask went around to each fox hole telling every man to be alert, because there are VC in the parameter.

I then heard footsteps coming in my direction to our

fox hole. I wanted to see the person's face before I fired, because I wanted to make sure I didn't miss when I fired my weapon.

I said, Halt! Who's there? No one answered, Halt! Who's there? No one answered. I then removed the slack out of the trigger of my M–16, and I was ready to fire at will. I did not know, if it was someone from the company or if it was a VC trying to find out if American soldiers were on this side of the parameter.

Then I heard a voice that cried out, Joe!, Joe! this is Robert! I said, I see you, come out to your right. I asked Robert, why didn't you answer me? I called out to you twice, Who's there. He said, I couldn't hear, I lost my hearing after firing the M–90, Joe! Are you guys all right?

Then I jumped up and said, Robert, if you didn't call my name, I would have shot and killed you. Robert said, I am glad you waited and heard your name or I would have been shot for sure or killed by you. We just laughed a little then Robert informed us the gun ships had come to help us out. Pop some smoke to mark this side of the parameter for the gun ships.

Robert then left and was on his way to the CP. After about fifteen artillery rounds were fired, the helicopter gun ships arrived. You could see them this time as they went into action. They flew up high in the sky and then turned on a bright light, as they dived like a jet fighter.

The helicopters started firing their grenades, M–60 rounds, launching rockets down upon the VCs, as they moved the VC quickly from our parameter, backing them up to run across the border. The VC body count was heavy from this battle.

These two gunners (one was a brother), flew these choppers really great,. They have on occasion been shot down by the VC, either by bow and arrow or small weapon fire. We again suffered losses: six killed and four wounded. The Cambodian border had reduced our company size, according to the number of men left in each platoon.

The 2nd platoon was down to ten guys and needed replacements if we planned to survive another attack from the VCs. After hearing that Stucky was dead, I cried, because he was so close to going home, and never made it. Four weeks left in country, and he and Andy are both dead now! What a waste! What would my future hold?

Because I got along with Stucky more then he did with anyone else, they gave Stucky's blue radio to me. Around 7:30 A.M. that morning we saddled up to sweep the area, checking for VC bodies, dead or alive.

This time we were caught off guard, when we found out that this battle early this morning was against the VC women unit. They were killed, nice-looking; this was a waste. I thought women always said they were smarter than men. Not if they decided to fight in a senseless war; they can die, too.

Many of the guys were upset, because of Stucky and Andy's death, having had so little time left in country and the commander would not allow them to remain in Cu-Chi. We all felt that this was wrong and we were going to make sure, when we were short, that we would not be still fighting in this jungle.

The VC that was killed next to the tree, was dragged to the tree and a Wolfhound crest was stamped in his forehead. The Wolfhounds have been known to even remove VC body parts like ears, hands, and fingers; this was one of the reasons for the thousand-dollar bounty on the Wolfhound's head.

This was what someone had done. I felt that it was not called for. Yes, he was a dead VC, but we did not need to mistreat his body. We got ourselves together. The 2nd platoon went out on a sweep to recon the area to see if there was any activity to the south of our parameter.

We returned to the company location, 2nd and 1st platoon with no known news of VC activity to the south of our parameter. The guy that was short, Robert Brown, went back to Cu-Chi with the wounded soldiers to spend his 20 days in a more secure area. He would make it home.

The rest of us complained to the Captain and First Sergeant about short times being in the field after the death of Stucky and Andy. That's why Robert Brown went in; it was okayed by the Captain to do this for the soldiers.

That night as we pulled guard duty we wondered if the VC were going to attack us again. It was a cool night but nothing was taken for granted in this war. Sir Charles had it hard and would fight with all his might. It would be nice to be home about right now. I know if my family knew what I've been though these past few days they would start their own war with the Pentagon.

The next day was Thanksgiving. They had flown food and additional troop replacements to our location, increasing the manpower and fire power to help defend this parameter. Thanksgiving was lonely and sad, due to all the gunfiring and the dead soldiers. American or Viet Cong, dead is dead. We continued smelling the guns and artillery rounds' gun powder for days; it had permeated the air.

We remained there for three more days and finally received the barbed wire we had requested four days earlier, before the second battle. The barbed wire could have prevented the VC from overrunning the parameter, but who cares. The Commanders in Cu-Chi just wanted a body count, ours or the VC, a body count.

After staying on the border for three more days, the helicopters arrived on the third day to pick up all of the additional supplies that we could not carry or no longer needed to perform our recon sweep.

Spending eleven days on the Cambodian border cut many of our teeth for the old old timers and us new old timers. This had to have been the worst yet that Alpha company had seen.

Our last night on the Cambodian border we saw a fire fight. We were later informed that it was Charlie company from our battalion that was in battle with the VC. You saw tracers going in and out of the parameter, then you heard that familiar sound that only a helicopter gun ship could make.

It sounded like a herd of elephants running, and making sounds with their mouths as the gun ship dropped their rockets, grenades, and fired their M–60 machine guns. Even though Charlie company was about five miles away, the picture was clear and the pressures they were under, far too familiar.

Charlie company's battle with the VCs lasted about three to four hours, they had suffered great losses. Madlock, a friend of Ed's and me, was in Charlie company, and both Ed and I could only think and hope that Madlock was not among the casualties.

Explosions sounded like the fourth of July, as I thought to myself, "Why were we here?" So, that eleventh day, we were eagle flown back to Diamond II, to remain there until additional replacements increased the size of each platoon; before we took on another big mission.

While reconning the area around Diamond II, we could not help but notice dead VC bodies and the smell of those that were dead. Either they had run, as far as they could, or the other VC could no longer carry them any further. The bodies were left where the sun and weather conditions exposed the bodies. Now all the insects had taken advantage of this opportunity of the dead.

There were signs, written in Vietnamese, that said "kill zone," so our eyes were focused to locate any booby traps to be exploded, or an ambush somewhere. We found many booby traps that we exploded, on that day.

This was a two-day overnight ambush patrol for our platoon. We had C-rations for two meals or just some fruit until we made it back from this two-day recon.

We slept in the different location each night, to spring a ambush on Sir Charles if he came this way. We had been back from the border for about a day and we got a two-day overnight patrol; no bath or shower in all this time. Maybe we brushed our teeth once or twice and now we would not have a hot meal until we returned in two days.

That two-day's patrol went okay. We didn't see anyone and if they saw us they did not want to fight; they must have passed us by. That next morning after the last men pulled their guard duty, they told everyone to get up so we could take up our claymore mines and trap flares, then prepare ourselves for the recon and sweep back to Diamond II. We left our night location that morning about 6:45 A.M., to make it back to Diamond II before 10:00 A.M. if possible.

In the meanwhile, Alpha company were at Diamond II, licking our wounds to heal them. Two days later new replacements finally arrived. Harry from Chicago, Doc Brown also from Chicago by way of New Mexico, and Joe G. from Atlanta, Georgia. These three brothers and about six Caucasians were added to our company.

As we walked though the front gates of Diamond II and headed to our assigned bunkers we saw some new faces but wanted to take off our gear, then eat and find out who these new guys were and what platoon they would be assigned too.

After we ate, Ed and I met all of the new guys and welcomed them to the company and the other three to our platoon. Doc Brown was part of the CP, because he was a medic, and would only remain in the field for eight months, much like the officers, who spend six months in the field.

Four days later we received new orders and Alpha company (Wolfhounds) had to go to Ta-Nang, which was the area we had been reassigned to in December, 1968. They wanted us to let Sir Charles know that we didn't play games with him.

X

The Tet Offensive at Christmas Time

The Hornets chopper pilots arrived the next morning, ready to take us to Ta-Nang. This new location was currently manned by the 1st Calvary Unit, but they found it difficult keeping Sir Charles from shooting their guns and RPG rounds at them every day. Now we had to stop Sir Charles. We arrived at this location about ten o'clock that morning. Then the unexpected happened to me, which I still don't understand, even now.

Our mission was to secure the area, do some police action in the community, and run Sir Charles out of town. It sounds like a small order, not too hard to do correctly. Just listen.

We would have the opportunity to guard a smaller parameter, because of our company size, and be able to received additional troops when they became available. We had started our descent to the location in the choppers. One by one the choppers landed; everyone jumped off, the 1st Calvary hopped on the choppers. The Hornets were ready to take off.

Everyone noticed that the 1st Calvary had set up their camp parameter in a cemetery. That was strange for me; I could not understand their using a cemetery, purposely, for a battleground. I guess if we got killed, we were already there with the dead. I don't know why they set up here.

As the 1st Calvary Unit climbed on board the choppers, they wished us the best and hoped we would be able to deal with the VCs better than they had. Ed and I had walked into the parameter of the 1st Calvary, along with some of the other guys, in our company, as the 1st Calvary was still gathering their gear.

I spotted something silver in the cemetery soil, but I've been told not to pick anything up, so I didn't. Ed, seeing that they were dog tags, immediately did so. Ed and I asked the guys in 1st Calvary if the dog tags were any of theirs. They said, No, we have ours, see. And they took them out and showed them to us.

Then Ed said, Maybe it's one of the guys in 1st Calvary that went out of the gate, whose name is on the dog tags. Ed, I said, What's the name? Ed said, It says "Joseph Smith," Well, they are yours, you must have dropped them once we reached this spot.

I said, No, both of mine are taped together and they are still on the chain around my neck. Ed said, Let me see these dog tags. So he looked at the two dog tags. He compared them to the other two I had around my neck.

It was then, though, as if I had gotten killed. This could not be, because Ed and others were talking to me. I said then, Now could someone have the same name, same U.S. number? Something was wrong. So Ed returned all four dog tags to me and said, I don't know what to say. That's strange to have the same U.S. number and all the rest of that information.

As I sat there, our demo man started placing shape charges and claymore mines in the direction that 1st Calvary identified to be the area from which they received mortal rounds. There was a hooch about 500 feet from the front gate that we kept an eye on, because it provided good cover for the VC, if they were going to use it.

Again, it looked like we were going to spend Christmas in the field, much like our Thanksgiving, because this was the 19th of December, 1968, and we had just arrived.

As I wondered, about the dog tags, if something had happened or was going to happen, I then placed the other two dog tags around my neck, taping all four together.

We then went out to recon the area. We swept, going eastward, as the 3rd platoon swept to the south. This was done so we could get a feel for the area, to fortify our defense of our parameter.

We found some old French ruins, because at one time the French ruled over Vietnam. We had also located some of their booby traps that were blown by our demo man. There was a village occupied by mothers and their daughters. We checked the village to see if Sir Charles was there in hiding, or if there were young men between the age of 14 and 45 in the village.

After not finding any VC or young men in the village, we left to continue our recon to secure the road that was used to bring us supplies. It also allowed the people in the village to travel on it. This road had to be swept by a mine sweeper each day, so no one traveling this road would have their vehicle blown up by a mine.

The first evening about 6:00 P.M., RPG rockets, mortar rounds, and small weapon fire hit our camp, with one RPG round landing next to the mess hall tent and the other RPG round overshooting the parameter.

Our mortar platoon returned fire, back into the thick-hedged roll, which was where the gunfire came from. Then they stopped. The Captain had radioed the artillery unit in Cu-Chi and this unit had the artillery rounds zinging through the air blowing up the bamboo-hedged roll.

As many more artillery rounds were fired, they walked the rounds further into the heavy tree area. After ten minutes of artillery shelling, it was stopped and the VC remained peaceful until the next day.

They shot an RPG round, which overshot the parameter. Just then, 3rd platoon detonated the shape charge they had placed in front of their bunker the day before. It became quiet and it remained like that, for days.

The mortar unit did not like the idea of that hooch 500 feet in front of our parameter. They took some C–4 the next morning and burned the hooch down. No one lived there, so the Captain gave his okay.

We met two young ladies from the village that spoke to us as we guarded the road with caution. We wondered if they were sent by the VC to count how many troops were there, and identify our position location to the enemy.

Little children would come out to sell soda, at fifty cents a can, when soda only cost fifteen cents at home in the U.S. Some of the little boys were selling their sisters for money in order to have food, so their family could survive.

As each day went on, we would receive sniper gunfire, but no one has ever been injured from it. Each platoon had their turn doing night patrol, camping out all night until morning. Then they would return to the camp parameter, after they recon, as they swept the area on their way back into the camp parameter.

One night, my platoon had to do night patrol. It was bad, because the moon was out, meaning it was very bright that night. It was a few days before Christmas; we had just received a new gun-hole sergeant, who fit the expression "wanted to be the hero thinking that this war was a television series and this was his part in the movies."

I told him to be cool, but one thing I have come to realize in my life; some Caucasian people do not want to listen to any African-Americans, no matter how much experience the African-American has.

Caucasians must feel that they are in control, even at the expense of their life. This is sad, but true. I know the way Caucasians were taught is different from the way that African-Americans were taught, to the point that I wonder if they were taught respect, to love and to help one another. This has been our culture, its foundation, taught to the African-American people. Sometimes I felt bad for the Caucasian people because they did not receive the discipline that we have to help them mature. They are still at age ten.

Peter replaced the sergeant in our platoon due to the other sergeant having received injuries at the Cambodian border battle. Peter was just like a kid in a candy store, he wanted action, and now! So Rick said, Look Sarg, Joe told you to be cool. You better listen to this guy; you haven't seen any action yet, you don't want to see any either.

That night, as Peter pulled guard duty, Peter was snoring as though he were at home in his bed. I shook him, then told him that he was making too much noise as he slept. He said, Okay. Within a few minutes he was doing it again, snoring that is, so I woke him up and he said, How am I supposed to get any sleep? You'll have to sleep back in camp in the morning, because if you continue sleeping like this, Sir Charles will not need to cut your throat, I will.

We were out in the open, with no perimeter cover. This was Lieutenant Nebask's idea, because he was afraid of going in the hedged roll to receive proper camouflage from Sir Charles.

The Lieutenant started snoring, so I crawled over to where he was, woke him up, and told him to stop making that noise as he slept. I was so glad when morning finally arrived. I had been a nervous wreck all night, because of these two stupid people that could not stay awake to save their life.

When you're on guard duty, you must stay awake to watch out and make sure that the enemy does not crawl up on you. The guard warned the others to get ready because of the activity advancing towards us. This could not be done if everyone was asleep, including the person pulling guard duty.

That morning both the Lieutenant and the Sergeant (Peter) jumped down my throat after we were in the field camp parameter. I told them both, The next time I will not awaken you. With my hand I'll just slice your throat, understand? You're not at home and we need every able body to defend one another, if we are under attack. This is Vietnam, let me remind both of you, and neither you (Peter) nor the Lieutenant will cause me to lose my life, because you both want to sleep. I suggest you both think about what I just said, before our next mission.

I walked away angry enough that I could have shot them both for thinking so stupidly. Many of the guys told me to forget it, let's get some rest for the bunker guard duty tonight.

That night I was assigned to a bunker on the north side of the parameter to guard all night by myself, because of what I had said to the Lieutenant and the Sergeant. This is what I mean when I said that the Lieutenant did not think. If I become tired and fall asleep, that just might be the point of entry that Sir Charles will take because they would not see anyone on guard duty. So with one man guarding this bunker, the rest of the company could be killed because of poor defense.

About fifteen minutes after I had arrived at the bunker, Joe G. and Willie came down to see me. They said, we'll pull guard duty with you. Just then the Lieutenant showed up and asked, Joe G. and Willie, why did you come over to this bunker? Before either of them could answer, the Captain came out of the CP and announced that it had been reported that there's heavy activity in the area; VC movement.

I always wonder, Was it VC movement or had the Captain heard what happened on the 2nd platoon night patrol and found out that the Lieutenant placed me on a bunker by myself? Could that have been the reason for the VC movement?

The Captain said, three to four men to a bunker. The Lieutenant looked at me, turned, and walked away. You see how good God is, turning the tables to protect me from unjust punishment.

Ed joined us at this bunker and we were ready for the action from Sir Charles, if any was coming. We kind of talked to each other all night, with the person on guard, and the rest. The shelling from the artillery did make it a little hard to sleep; that was one of the reasons we just kept each other company this entire night.

The next morning, 2nd and 3rd platoon reconned the area, sweeping to find Sir Charles. This was the area the activity would have been in on last night. We saddled up and moved out of the parameter, and into the village area. As we approached the village we noticed that no one was there; the artillery from last night had forced the people in the village to flee for cover.

We spread out, searching the village. Then the Lieutenant and I entered a hooch. Just as soon as the Lieutenant sat down in a chair, shots rang out, hitting plates in the hooch. I got down, but I was unable to return gunfire, because a few of our guys were in my field of fire.

The Lieutenant got up to run. Gunfire rang out again; he fell down. I then crawled to the other side, where I was able to see where the VC was shooting from. He was in the rice field. I said, Yates, he's 200 feet to your left. Yates placed an HE round in his M–79 grenade launcher, then fired.

The round went beyond the target. I called to him again. Yates, too far! I yelled, Walk it back. Yates fired again.

This time it must have landed five feet away from the target.

I then called for rear support from our mortar platoon. They fired three rounds, but the VC had moved after Yates had fired his last round. The Lieutenant and I got up off of the floor of the hooch to check the area.

Our platoon then moved out of the area in pursuit of this VC, because there were women and young girls in the rice fields about a thousand feet away and we did not return as much gunfire, because we might have hit them.

As we started moving out, we spotted this guy running. I called out Stop! Then Ed fired his M–60 in the air; the boy stopped. It may have been a diversion in order for the real VC to get away by switching clothes with this boy.

Joe G., another guy, and myself then ran over to where this guy was, keeping our weapons pointed at him at all times. Then I searched him and noticed the bars on his shoulders. He was a VC major. I also found a pearl-handled Russian .45 pistol under his shirt, stuck in the back of his pants along with a map.

A couple of Caucasian guys asked me if I was going to keep this gun. I told them that I was not sure. We then waited for the rest of the platoon; then the Lieutenant called Alpha 6 and reported that we had caught a VC major.

As 2nd platoon escorted the VC major back to our camp parameter, 3rd platoon was carrying Lieutenant Johnson, who had stepped on a booby trap. You could hear him saying, through his pain and tears, Million dollar wound! Whoo,whoo,wee, million dollar wound! Whoo,whoo,wee.

We posted a couple of guys around the VC major. I went over to find out how bad Lieutenant Johnson's injuries were: scrap metal in his legs and stomach. Lieutenant Johnson told me to tell his Vietnamese wife that he would be going to the hospital in Cu-Chi, and he didn't know how long he would remain in Cu-Chi before they flew him back to the States. The helicopter then arrived to take the VC major and Lieutenant Johnson to Cu-Chi. The VC major would be interrogated to give us locations and other information if he was an officer and had important information.

Even though we had one less Lieutenant patrolling, our night ambushes still continued to ensure that the pressure remained on the VC in this area, letting them know that the Wolfhounds were not to be easily moved.

Two days later, Lieutenant Johnson's wife came to the gate and asked for me. I went to the gate and told her what the Lieutenant had instructed me to. She put her head in her hands, then lifted her head with tears in her eyes. I told her to go see him and be careful traveling the roads. She then left for Cu-Chi. I did not know if she would be able to enter the base camp or not. Maybe, because the Lieutenant was her husband.

That night 2nd platoon had an ambush patrol. It was dark, so we held on to each other's clothing and hoped that Sir Charles did not join the ranks, where he might overtake us. We would not have been aware of his presence until someone made a sound.

We never knew who would return to our LP parameter, when someone went out to set up his claymore mines and trip flares. The VC could have killed the guy that was setting up his claymore mine and trip flares and returned in his place, to kill those in the parameter.

I prayed to God to keep the persons on guard awake, but I then saw someone walking by, touching or stabbing as he went by each man. I woke Joe G. and told him to get ready, that if this guy was a "gook" we were going to go down fighting.

Thank God, it turned out that this guy was touching the other guys, because he was trying to find the next guy to pull guard duty. Joe G. and I remained up for the rest of the other person's guard duty.

The next morning we rewound our claymore lines, but had to use caution removing them, because Sir Charles could have slipped up during the night and booby trapped the claymore mines. Because some guys fell asleep on guard duty, that would have been the time for Sir Charles to rig the claymore mines.

Sir Charles was slick; you never cut him any slack at all. He was protecting his home and we knew not why we were there. So we saddled up and began our sweep back to the parameter.

After we arrived back to our parameter we had breakfast, thanking God for another day. We went on mission after mission. Every day it was a little different, but with much humbleness did I walk.

Would you know, Christmas is just like any other day in Vietnam. So was Monday to Sunday; we never knew what day or date it was until the end of the month. We received our paychecks; great, we are going to party in the jungle.

Oh yeah, every man had about five or ten dollars of MPC (Military Payment Currency) that they could spend on soda purchased from the Vietnamese children, which we were instructed not to do. I would get money orders and mail my checks to my brother Warren, to help him with his college education.

The money didn't do me any good in the field, especially at Christmas time. You see, I kept one hundred dollars and I bought a smoking jacket for my father, a mama-san pajamas set for my step-mother, and some other items to send home to my brothers and sisters. All of these items cost me twenty-five dollars, no postal charge. Ha-Ha!

Well it was Christmas night and the Tet-Offensive was an act of VC moving around setting up attack ambushes. That night, 2nd platoon had to go on night patrol. With two new guys added to our platoon, it was a spooky night.

The area we moved through had trees uprooted and they were turned on their side from artillery rounds and the looks of a few bomb strikes in this same location. Once we left the parameter, we were receiving sniper gunfire in our general direction, but the sniper did not know where we were.

Every ten to fifteen minutes the sniper would fire his weapon, trying to draw fire from us, but it was very dark; that was why the sniper (VC) could not make us out to be a true target for him or her.

We finally reached an area where we were going to set up our guard post for that night. Then the sniper fired his weapon again. He must have been about 200 meters away when the two new guys turned their weapons to fully automatic, returning gunfire, as did many of the other nervous guys.

I grabbed both of these new guys. I felt like killing them both, for giving our position away. At the same time Lieutenant Nebask and I were yelling to have everyone stop firing their weapons.

After getting everybody under control I told Lieutenant Nebask that we needed to move about 200 meters from this site. We waited for 30 minutes, then moved out to a new location after checking with the Captain at our CP. It was okayed by the Captain. They told us artillery had to remark their firing pattern to ensure our location was not marked for HE rounds, because friendly forces were not in this location initially.

There wasn't any activity all night. We were sure that an attack would take place because Sir Charles now knew that we were in this location. But the next morning after we had saddled up and walked about 300 meters, a couple of RPG rockets landed in our first LP location site. I gave God the thanks for putting it in my mind, to tell the Lieutenant to move to another location.

Even if we had remained in the first location all night and left in the morning, the scrapped metal from the RPG rockets would have wounded a few guys based on the distance we would have traveled from that location.

We looked back and took cover after the first rocket exploded then waited. The other rocket then exploded. It was quick; our company CP called us Alpha 2 over. I returned the call: Alpha 6 this is Alpha 2 over, Alpha 6 copy give me the status. Then I told the Captain, in code, that we were okay, but the first night post was hit by RPG rockets. He copied and out I rogered that out.

After we returned to the camp parameter and ate breakfast, Miller, Joe G., Willie, Ed, and I wanted to wash up and wash our clothes. It had been about eight weeks and our bodies had not seen water since the stand down after the bridge blew up early November. Everybody needed to be down wind of each other.

There were women in the rice fields as we began washing ourselves, one guy pouring water on the other. We then started washing our clothes, placing them on our bunkers to be dried by the sun within 30 minutes. Everybody's clothes were dried but mine when shots rang out; Bom! Bom! Ta-Ta-Ta-Ta-Ta gunfire. The Lieutenant told us to saddle up. My clothes were wet and I did not want to die, without any clothes on.

So my platoon left me. I grabbed my wet clothes and put them on, threw on my gear, and cautiously tried to find my platoon. The Captain said that I should stay, but I felt I needed to be with my platoon in a fire fight.

Up ahead, about 100 meters I saw the guy that was bring up the rear of my platoon. I got his attention by softly calling, "Rick" as quietly as I could, without them thinking that I was Sir Charles and shooting me. I then took my position as RTO, as we continued sweeping the area.

There was a jeep with two American soldiers in it. Some guy had told them not to go down this road unless we were guarding it. They said, It's not dark yet, and they left when they should have returned, the way they came.

We heard two RPG rockets explode. One rocket hit the fuel tank of the jeep, and the other hit the side of the jeep. Both men were dead. We secured the area and asked papa-san if he had seen any VC. He said no.

The helicopter arrived about 20 minutes after we called it in to pick up the two dead men. They never knew what hit then. Their bodies were burned somewhat, from the jeep fuel tank that exploded. Scrapped metal pierced their bodies, as they laid on the ground with their bodies twisted and crushed from the weight of the jeep, as it rolled over them, in flames.

Because the jeep was blown up with the two men in it, our platoon set fire to the hooches near the burning jeep. Afterward mama-san and papa-san said they had seen nothing. Then we spotted someone running; we started to fire our M–16s, which brought down a VC who was running away.

After this event, the new guys were steaming mad. There was one guy that was Caucasian and American-Indian who carried a bowie knife. He wanted action. They started burning the hooches as we swept the area for more VCs.

He was really good with his knife, but in time his bravery would melt away. The Captain informed us by radio that we needed to remain out there with the 3rd platoon who would set up their ambush site on the north side; ours would be on the south side.

Our ambush patrol that night was a dried up rice field. This was selected for our first ambush site. That night I thought, for your twelve years of education, you received a weapon and no information about dying. Do you really think they care? No. If they did, they would have sat down and talked about how to work out this war conflict, without the loss of lives, which they finally did in 1975.

No; the only thing that they wanted to do was to save face. But for whom? They just did not care about you being 19, even though you were just getting ready to start your life. People have told me, you're young and you don't know anything. So I prayed. I guess that must have been because most of the adults had a lot of debt, and the U.S. felt it was more important for the older people with families to remain at work and send the children to fight for them. (They just don't have the right to make decision for the country; they're too young.)

The next morning we returned to our parameter, had breakfast and were assigned to pull guard duty on the bunker line that night. That night, a trip flare went off on the east side of the bunker line. Everyone started firing their weapons, as some shot off additional aerial flares to illuminate the area; to see what or whom, had set the trip flare off. It was a rabbit.

Even the rabbit was safe on that side of the parameter; it just hopped away. After the shooting had stopped, we could see the rabbit hopping down the rice dice from the light of the flares.

Later that night in a distance, gunfighting was heard. We could hear and see that someone else was in a heated battle. There was a battle with the VCs and the U.S. about 4 miles from our location. We could hear the booms! and the bams! throughout the night. It was too hard for me to sleep, due to a battle situation.

It was around the first week of January of 1969. I had full charge of an LP unit, when there were reports of heavy activity moving in our direction. Lieutenant Nebask didn't care that much for me and I didn't care too much for his attitude; he just wanted me to carry the radio and not talk. Just give me the horn, that's what the Lieutenant told me.

I was not going to find him if we were a distance from each othe, if we encountered any battle, just to let him talk on the radio. He needed to find someone else to be the RTO, someone that would jump when he said to.

The Lieutenant was truly more afraid than I realized. He would have nightmares, thinking that the VC were all around him, and wake up at night, yelling and screaming. Stop! stop! Don't kill me! That is what he would say in his sleep.

That night Lieutenant Nebask told me to select seven men to go on the night patrol. He said, I bet no one would want to go out of this parameter with a bigmouth like you. I told him maybe not; and my name is not bigmouth, it's Joseph Robert. He said, It's Lieutenant to you. He said, if no one goes you'll be out there by yourself. Well, God had our whole platoon asking me to take them with me, but I only took seven men. That was all I needed, seven.

The Lieutenant was really upset and asked, why no one volunteered to go on patrol with him. They said, Because you'll only think of yourself; Joe thinks about us first, always. I told them that it was crazy to send me out there with these seven guys, when there is a report of one to two battalions of VC moving in this area. But we still had to go.

We left the parameter by notifying the CP in code that we were leaving. I took the patrol about 500 meters out in front of our bunker line to watch for VC movement. I didn't know how we would make it back in the parameter if we spotted VC movement. We were to be sacrificed for the company safety, but a change took place after we were out there for three hours.

A message was radioed to us from the CP, telling us to return to the parameter immediately. I then woke up the other guys and we pulled up our claymore mines and trip flares, and we started walking back to the parameter. I took the rear support to ensure that no one would be left behind. Our parameter shot aerial flares, lighting our way back to the parameter. Once we had returned, I took roll call to make sure all were present and accounted for.

Every man was assigned to a bunker. As I pulled my hour of guard duty, I noticed through the star-light-scope two men (maybe VC) smoking something other than cigarettes. It was difficult to sleep that night, so everyone at my bunker kind of kept each other company or we all pulled guard duty until morning.

Just before the morning mess call, gunfire rang out. We returned gunfire to the area, in front of the 3rd platoon bunkers line. We then quietly saddled up to recon the area looking for this VC. Many of the guys were upset and so they burned down some more of the people's hooches, as we moved through the village area.

After we completed our recon sweep of the area and did not find this VC who shot at us that morning, we returned to the parameter to have our breakfast and do some other work around the parameter. Many of the hooches and hedged rolls close to our parameter were cut down, giving us a wide area for our field of fire.

Many of the people in the village were upset because

we destroyed their burial grounds, and then we upset their dead, just to build our bunkers. Maybe this was part of the reason that 1st Calvary had a hard time, because they were in their cemetery.

Headquarters then notified our Captain to have us move out of that area to a new location on the hill, currently manned by a engineering unit. So we took all the bunkers down, emptied out all the sand bags, and moved up to the hill. After we had relocated, our platoon had night patrol. We set up in a cemetery, no cover, just the head stone.

Sometimes I felt that the Lieutenant was off his rocker putting us out in the open like that. If we were under attack, one RPG rocket would have wiped most of the platoon out. On nights like this, you jump for joy when morning comes.

I was lying on top of somebody's grave and was trying to find cover between the two bumps in the ground made by the bodies beneath it. In an open area like this, we were like sitting ducks waiting to be shot down by the VC.

The moon, that night, seems to have been brighter than ever before. It lit our position well, in favor of the VC. That night I told Peter, the Sergeant, not to fall asleep on guard duty; that if he did, I would slit his throat.

I then pulled the poncho liner over my head, but peeked from under it and could not help from noticing that no one was pulling guard duty. Peter was fast asleep, snoring, unaware of where he was. I woke him up and told him to stay awake, as quietly as I could. He replied, yea!, yea!, yea, okay.

No sooner had I pulled the poncho liner over my head the second time, than Peter had fallen back to sleep. Boy, you could see the redness in my face, even though it was night. I pulled my knife from my holder, then crawled to were Peter was. Placing the knife at his neck, I told him to get up. I quietly told him, Sir Charles will not wake you; I did this time, this is how people die, because of stupidity on your part. Now stay awake!

Peter put his hands around his neck, frightened from my knife on his throat. He then awakened the next person to pull their guard shift once he completed his hour.

The next morning as we were saddling up, Peter told me that I had better not ever do that again. I said, I won't, because the next time I will kill you. Your life depends on me and my life depends on you; therefore, sleeping on guard duty will kill everyone.

It had turned into a shouting match for a few seconds. Many of the other guys tried to tell Peter that he must be responsible and think of the rest of us out there. Then I said, I won't warn you, I'll just cut your throat.

We then started our recon of the area. As we moved toward the camp parameter, there was a village 500 meters to our front. We saw black pajamas moving in the village area. One of the new troops pointed his weapon. I was six guys in front of this troop. I turned and said, Don't shoot, there is no weapon; the troop had fired his gun, but I got to him before he fired the next round. But he fired his weapon; I had pushed up the barrel of his M–16, which projected the bullet in the air.

I then pulled the guy, removed the M–16 from his hands, and told him that you need to know when to shoot and when not to. She was running for her baby, but you just wanted to shoot your weapon anyhow to kill someone. The troop dropped his head and said that he didn't know what to do. I said, That's why us old-timers are here; follow our lead.

We then moved towards the target, the platoon spreading out to cover the area. Then we came upon the women. The troop shot her in the hip from the first shot fired from his M–16. A couple of the other troops, went over to the village with caution, to get the lady's young child.

She did not speak any English so I spoke to her and explained that it was an accident that she was shot, because she was thought to be a Viet Cong. She said, repeatedly, No Viet Cong! No Viet Cong! I said that it was all right, but some of the other guys had taken come show to burn her hooch.

The flames started to blaze then she yelled that her son (boy-san) was in the hooch bunker. Two of the soldiers brought him out of the hooch. They threw water on the hooch that was in flames to put the fire out.

Her son was between the ages of twelve and fourteen, which made him a likely candidate to be a VC or a part of the Vietnamese army. So we brought him in for interrogation and she went to receive medical treatment. Our medic applied a bandage to stop the bleeding, but the bullet had to be removed.

The woman had done well for this long keeping her son out of the war. The interrogation uncovered nothing, but they remained in Cu-Chi for a few days and were returned to their home by convoy in a week.

We saw them every now and then, as we reconned and swept the area near their village. One day, before the road had been swept by the mine squad, this little Vietnamese motor car, with two boys and a lovely young lady, were coming up the road.

After we saw them, we tried to tell them, Stop, the road might be mined. Just then, they hit a mine 200 meters from our front gate. That motor car went up then came down so fast, turning over once it touched the ground.

One boy was seriously injured from the scrapped metal. The young lady had a broken ankle, and the other boy had bruises, with some small fragments of scrapped metal in his arms and legs.

With caution, this mine squad went out, carefully checking for more mines, as the medic attended to the wounded Vietnamese. The medical helicopter soon arrived to transport the wounded lady and boys to the hospital in Cu-Chi. The area was secured before the helicopter arrived. The CP had to radio for medic-vac after the explosion.

XI

Who's Afraid of Walking Point?

The patrolling and guarding the road was not all that bad, but was not as good as the guard duty we had while on the Phu-Vinh bridge. Now we were in the field, with just water for drinking, and C-rations for two meals. Sometimes we had to spend days away from the field base camp parameter trying to find the VCs.

Yes, body odor, wet feet, bad breath, little to eat, and very little to no sleep at all. My sunglasses and regular glasses, I no longer had; scrapped metal and bullets destroyed them, in my sleeping area, while on the Cambodian border.

I had requested new glasses, but it takes awhile, maybe six or eight months. I found myself closing my eyes a great deal during the daylight hours, but was able to see much better once I pulled my helmet down to block the brightness of the sunlight from my eyes.

I managed to do the best I could with what I had to work with and the limits I had to work under in the army and in Vietnam. After we returned to our parameter from the three-day mission we rested only to go out the next day on another patrol.

Before it became night we received a radio call (CP) that there was movement in our area. We saddle up to move into this area, which was about one mile from our parameter. Gunfire rang out, and as we moved back to our parameter, two guys moved to the other side of the hooch, as the VC continued firing at us.

Then the guys were about 75 feet away from the hooch. They opened fire on the VC. One of our guys fired his M–79 grenade launcher HE round that hit one VC in the head, and the other VC was shot by M–16 gunfire. Both of the VC were dead. The third VC was captured and was taken in for interrogation. This hooch was then burned down by some of the troops.

We then took the VC back to our camp parameter. A helicopter would be on its way to pick up the VC and take him to the interrogation office at Cu-Chi. We had our supper and pulled our guard duty on the bunker line that night. There was a cool breeze blowing that night as I looked through the star-light-scope to check if Sir Charles was making his move, but morning finally arrived.

Everyone gets an opportunity to walk point: the Captains, Lieutenants, and the medic are the only ones not permitted to have this honor. Yea, all right. Well, this morning it was my turn. I had more guys volunteering to walk point in my place than one could have ever thought.

This had always given Lieutenant Nebask problems. Why would Caucasians volunteer to do something for Joe? But they would tell him, Joe is a real person and he has gone to bat for us a lot. What have you done?

When we didn't have C-rations, Joe got them. When we didn't have clean clothes, Joe got them. When we needed something sent off home, Joe managed to get in to Cu-Chi to mail it. What have you done, Lieutenant Nebask?

Plus, Joe taught us how to survive out here That's your job Lieutenant, but you haven't done it. I said, Thank you fellows, as I moved nervously. "I prayed silently to God, to keep me, guard my foot steps, as I walked on this sweep, help me to move, with swiftness that I be not shot down without a fighting chance. Be with us all, Lord, in Jesus' name. Amen."

I had often read my military-issue bible. I was a junior deacon in the church I attended in Hartford, Connecticut. "The Greater Liberty Temple" was the name of my church. Bishop J. I. Wilken was the pastor of this church, which was small, but had believers who trusted in God.

I started out of the front gate with my M–16, ammo, two canteens of water, and a couple of cans of fruit from the C-rations box. We had to secure the road so that the convoy that would arrive later would not be ambushed.

We had to cover an area of about 5000 meters. Each day this had to be done, because each night Sir Charles would come out, set up mines in the road, and place booby traps in the village, tall grass, and hedged rolls.

It would be deadly if the mine sweep was not done routinely each day. I guess this can be compared to dead roll; the only difference is once we complete this sweep this day, we get the opportunity to do it again and again; also like Russian Roulette, until something does happen.

Anyway, I lifted up my feet, looking up, down, around, in front of me checking for trip wires used, with some booby traps or a raised area in the ground where a mine could be planted. I was twenty feet in front of the platoon, on the right and this other guy was off on the left. We kept eye contact with each other. We were 150 feet from each other.

If one of us spotted something we would lift up our hand to stop. Our platoon would stop moving forward, then everyone behind us would kneel down. There were a couple of hooches in front of me that had been partly destroyed, but enough of the hooch remained for someone to string a trip wire, making it a nice area to be booby trapped.

As I moved closer to that area, the morning sun reflected off something. So I raised my hand, stopping the entire platoon so I would be able to check out this object, without causing injury to the rest of the platoon. The platoon then squared down and the troops on my side faced outward. On the other side they faced outward to the left.

I moved closer to examine the object. I noticed that it was a trip wire. I then backed off, re-tracing my footsteps, and notified the first guy behind me to pass the word to have the demo man to come up. The demo man and I walked up to the area. I pointed to the trip wire, then I left him there to explode it.

I selected another route. The demo man advised me that we could move around the area and that he would set a long fuse before it would blow the mine. We had made it up the hill and then I saw the demo man running quickly. He had gotten about a hundred yards before yelling, Fire in the hole! Fire in the hole! The explosion went off.

He hit the dirt. One piece of scrapped metal went over his body as he laid in the dirt. He then got up and joined the rest of the platoon. We remained spread out to guard the road until about 6:00 P.M., when we started our return to our camp parameter.

One reason the Wolfhounds were wanted by the VCs, was because we would always call artillery and, if need be, an air strike. Trying to fight one-on-one was for the birds; plus this would reduce our chances of surviving in the jungle. Before we returned to our camp that evening we had taken a number of pictures with a camera. Everyone wanted a picture of themselves to send home to family and friends.

Later that month we received a Caucasian-American Indian that wanted to fight and see action, so I told him, You better hope we never return to the Cambodian border;

it's rough there, the VC regular army doesn't play.

We always received sniper fire; the VC would shoot two or three round then (dee-dee mow) run off. What we tried to do was place our shape charges out far enough so when we received sniper gunfire, we would detonate the shape charge, possibly hitting Sir Charles with fragments from the shape charge.

The shape charge did work. The next time that Sir Charles came around, it further reduced sniper gunfire for a few days. The weather was hot, but cool during the night; I guess from the rain during the day.

Ed, Joe G., Willie, and I built a sleeping bunker on the hill. We called it the "Soul Bunker." We had taken incense from some of the hooches during many of our recons and saved them. This was the ideal use for them in the "Soul Bunker."

We made five windows in this bunker, placing incense in each window. As the breeze blew the incense smoke around in the bunker, it kept the mosquitoes out. The bunker was hot, but the breeze that entered through the windows was nice as we slept in our black fishnet T-shirts. It wasn't home, but was far better than sleeping out in the open. Ed and I had been in country for three and a half months then, with 259 days left.

I was nineteen years old, but felt thirty-five because of the things that had happened and what I had seen up to then. It had matured us far beyond my years. Every man's responsibility, as well as my own rested upon my shoulders. Showers and clean clothes were something nice to have, but were not required out here.

Neither food, nor water took the top of the list, but staying alive meant more than anything. We told ourselves that many times a day. I had seen a lot by this point in Vietnam and felt real bad for the people in the village, because their food, daughters, sons, and husbands were taken by the VC or the village had been bombed by the U.S. They were in the middle of what ever happened here, not me.

We switched back and forward between the three platoons for road patrol, bunker duty, and night patrol. It was our turn, 2nd platoon, to go out on another mission, because 1st platoon was pulling the road patrol duty today and 3rd platoon just walked in the front gate. Third platoon would guard the bunkers all day and do the road patrol duty the next morning; that's how the rotation worked.

Our patrol LP for the night was going to be about one click (1 kilometer) from the camp parameter. Our platoon was 16 men strong and we had the fire power to handle most attacks from the local VC but this would not be the case on the border. The ammo would be gone too quickly in a heated battle.

We had set up this night mission in the center of this area where there was a rice field. About 250 feet on the east and west side of this rice field location, there were hedge rolls and an open field to the north and south.

The Lieutenant took an M–90 on this mission. We had been informed that there was heavy activity around this location, covering an area of about three to four miles in radius. He also had four bee-hive rounds and three HE rounds.

The night's activity was not bad. In fact, there was no activity at all. That was just great. There was a cool breeze blowing all night along with the dew, which made it a little cold. Morning arrived, after we pulled our night patrol. That morning, as we reconned the area back to our camp parameter, we spotted a young boy with a limp trying to get away from us. We immediately spread out and moved into the hooch and I caught him coming out of the back door entrance of the hooch.

His mother was yelling No VC! No VC! She did not want us to shoot him. So I asked him some questions and told his mother that he would be okay. I radioed the CP to inform them that we were bringing in a young Vietnamese boy.

We were not sure how he received his leg wound (scrapped metal). His mother said it was from a VC booby trap. The boy finally started talking; he spoke good English. So I instructed him to tell his mother that he would be back. We had to take him in for interrogation.

Once we arrived at our camp parameter and the Lieutenant informed the Captain that we found a boy in the village, the Captain had these Vietnamese soldiers interrogate the boy. After ten hours of interrogation, the Vietnamese soldiers stated that the boy was not a VC. He didn't know anything. He was then released to return home.

We continued our routine of rotation road patrol, overnight patrols, and guarding the bunker line until the Captain received a different assignment. Then came a mission. It would take place in two days; the company would eagle flight to a hot LZ. The activity was said to be heavy, so the entire 2nd Battalion (all four companies) met in this location to sweep this area.

I did not feel great the morning of our eagle flight to a hot LZ. I was afraid that I was going to die, so I told the Sergeant not to have me walk point. He said, If you don't, Joe G. or Willie will do it. So I said, Okay, I will do it.

The choppers took us to the location. It appeared to have been a very fast flight; we got off the choppers then secured the area. I took one look at the hedged roll and tears began to flow from my eyes.

I then turned to Willie, Joe G., Ed, Doc Brown, and Miller, and said, Will you guys have prayer with me?

They said Yes. So I prayed for myself, and every American that came on this mission and those fighting elsewhere in Nam.

After this prayer I felt alive and ready for anything, even if I had to return home in a body bag, I felt good then, on this day. As I started to walk, Joe G., Ed, Willie, Doc Brown, and Miller, all looked at one another. They hugged me. Then I saw that the point men for all the companies were African-American. My heart skipped a beat.

I just prayed silently to God for us point men that day, because of who we were, and how I felt America has treated African-Americans. As we walked through the thick hedged roll, the point men from each company would identify trip-wires or booby traps, when they saw one.

Then I heard an explosion. I said to myself, a brother must have stepped on a booby trap, but I kept walking, then finally we had reached the end of this hundred and fifty yard hedged roll.

I looked to my left, and there they were, all the others brothers, holding up their fists, giving up the power sign to one another. Thank God. I then raised my fist, with enjoyment jumping around in my body. I just smiled, with my tears.

Unbeknownst to me there was a booby trap about fifty feet in front of me on the rice paddy. As I started off walking again, the sun was directly in my face, so I stopped to bring my helmet down over my eyes, to block the sun. Then I noticed that there was a trip wire strung across the rice burn.

Then this little Caucasian Sergeant that was 2nd platoon tunnel rat, wanted to walk past Sergeant Williams to see if it was a booby trap. Sergeant Williams said, Where do you think you're going? This Sergeant said, To make sure there is a booby trap. Sergeant Williams told that Sergeant, if you don't get back in the ranks, you are going to lose your stripes.

Sergeant Williams said, Smith wait so everyone can step where you're stepping. I said, Okay. We all made it across the trip wire, having our demo man blow this booby trap up once everyone was a safe distance away.

The Major then came down from the sky in his loch helicopter, after Delta company had moved out of the area. Then it happened. The Major stepped on an in-ground booby-trap. (That's where the VC use a piece of wood with a nail through it, with the bullet end pointed up, to project it upward. Once the weight of the person pushes the bullet down on the nail, the nail strikes the back part of the bullet, like it's been fired from a gun.)

He was not killed, but I believe that it blew part of his foot off. The helicopter quickly went up to bring the Major to the hospital in Cu-Chi.

Some Lieutenant made a comment, that one of the grunts (meaning one of us soldiers) should have stepped on that booby trap and not the Major. The brothers that believed in God just said it was the Major's time to be wounded; maybe he'll respect the soldier more, because of his wound.

This all-day mission, which kept all the demo men busy from each company, blowing up the booby traps. We decided that it was time to eat our C-ration; it must have been around noon time. Once we finished eating, we continued our recon of the area until about 4:00 P.M. That was the time the choppers would arrive to pick us up to return us to our field base camp location.

After we had flown back to our camp, there was a hot meal waiting for us once we removed our gear. That night the rest of the company had the standard guard duty on the bunkers that outlines the size and depth of the parameter, with barbed wire that had three rolls of three wires high for each roll.

The 2nd platoon had to go on the overnight patrol mission, a mile or two in front of our field camp front gate. It was a little cool compared to the daytime temperature so we would use our poncho liner to help keep us a little warmer and reduce the amount of dew on us, because that would make us even colder, if we did not cover ourselves. Every man did his turn in pulling guard duty, including the Lieutenants and medics.

The Lieutenant and the Sergeant had not been snoring in their sleep and sleeping on guard duty anymore. Do you think the knife helped, I wonder? The next day was a stand-down day for our platoon because we had returned from our night patrol, after we returned from that all-day mission.

Supplies arrived, and we were able to wash our faces and brush our teeth. But there was not enough water to take a bath or wash up. So you had guys that had not had any water on their bodies since November, and some since the end of December. Maybe everybody needed a nose job just to forget the odor.

Because of all the heavy losses we had on the Cambodian border, our Sergeant was one that was also injured. With all of these new guys added to our platoon, we also received a new Sergeant, an E-6 named Williams. He was on the day mission with us and the entire Battalion.

Sergeant Williams was an African-American that had two children, and his wife in the photograph looked lovely. I asked him why he came to Vietnam, having a family. He said, To make more money to take care of my family. I said, What about another country, other than Nam? He said he would not receive as much pay as he would in Vietnam.

He was about 36 years old, with a great deal of care

and wisdom for all the men. He would risk his life for any one of us, if needed.

The Captain told Lieutenant Nebask that there was a report of movement to the north of our camp parameter. It was spotted by a recon helicopter a few days earlier. So much for our stand-down. We saddled up, two guys grabbed the M-60 bazooka, and we started out of the para meter.

The Lieutenant had switched his M-16 for a M-79 grenade launcher. He had accidentally taken the safety off when he put his gear on. As we continued our recon, the M-79 grenade launcher then fired the round. It landed three feet in front of me.

I did not know it until I lifted my head and saw it staring me in the face. Everyone thought the round was fired by the VC, because we heard the thumb, so we thought it was an RPG rocket that had been launched our way. That was the reason that everyone had got down on the ground; to protect themselves from the incoming round.

The HE M-79 round did not explode, thank God. It must travel fifteen feet in order to arm itself. I knew God was with me that day and was the only reason the round did not explode. I got up and said to Rob, the Lieutenant, What is wrong with you? Don't you know you're supposed to keep your safety on? He said, It is. I said, check it. He did.

The safety was off and just the shell remained in the chamber of his M-79. I told him, Why don't you get your M-16 back, because you can't shoot the M-79 grenade launcher that well. Stop playing games; I could have been killed, because of your carelessness.

I went up one side and down the other side of the lieutenant. He said nothing. He then looked at me and apologized! And apologized! and was sad about what had happened. The demo man then placed a charge of C–4 to blow the HE round that misfired from the M–79 grenade launcher.

As we continued our sweep of the area, we spotted a person running across the field. One of the guys shot and hit the person. Then we secured that area. A couple of guys went over to the person that was shot. A few of us searched the area next to the village.

The area I started to search had trees uprooted from artillery rounds and bomb strikes. As I walked slowly around the uprooted trees, I felt someone watching me. I turned to my left quickly. I saw something white dart back out of the doorway.

At that moment, I was upset and angry, fearful and was ready to kill. I had switched my weapon from safety to fully automatic, as I told him or her to come out with their hands up or I'd blow up that hooch. As he slowly walked out of the door, his hands were behind him.

I told him to lift your hands! I told him again, raise your hands! He stood there, as though he paid no mind to what I had said. I then fired a burst from my M–16 at his feet. Immediately the other guys ran over, when they heard the gunfire, to my location. I was going to kill this man if I had to shoot again.

I told them that this man did not want to come, and when I told him to raise his hands, he did not. That's when I fired my weapon, because his hands were behind him. I did not know if he had a gun or not. The other guys took him away to interrogate him along with mama-san, and the other lady that was wounded.

Later that evening the wounded woman was flown by helicopter into Cu-Chi for medical care with the man and the other women, where the three of them would be interrogated. The pressure was on to be on guard at all times, which always troubled me, because you never knew how to trust anyone there.

Ever since the two soldiers were blown up in the jeep on the road months ago, hooch-burning had increased from our platoon. When the people in the village did not tell us where Sir Charles was hiding, their hooch was burned down. If we had just received gunfire from the village area and they said nothing, their hooch would be burned down.

We searched the area and found a small supply of weapons. They would be returned to Cu-Chi by convoy the next day. Many times after we searched a village, we would receive sniper gunfire during the night, firing into the base camp parameter. We returned to the parameter before it was too dark out, to eat and pull guard duty on the bunker line.

The next day our company had to go out on a hot LZ. I was suppose to go, but Peter the Sergeant pleaded with me to let him go. I told him that this was real and I should go, but Ed and Joe G. also wanted to go. They wanted to keep me in the parameter.

Do you know how good God is? That people would think so much of God's people, that they would want to protect them? So they said, "Two-Four" that's what everyone called me. I gave in, and Joe G. and Peter the Sergeant went.

Ed and I guarded the bunker. The helicopters arrived and flew most of the company to this hot LZ. It must have been about 2 o'clock when the eagle flight returned to the camp parameter.

Joe G. said that Sergeant Williams and Peter the Sergeant were killed. Joe G. said, Once they got off the choppers and started moving into the area the VC opened fire. Peter never knew what hit him; he was dead. Sergeant

141

Williams was killed trying to get to Peter. Many of the other guys were wounded from this VC ambush.

The company was pinned down and was unable to move. Each time they did someone caught a bullet. I know that it was no one but God that kept Ed and me from going on this mission, and then we prayed.

The company tried to move back so the scrapped metal from the artillery rounds would not injure any more troops. After many rounds of artillery shells, the VC gun-firing had stopped. They then were able to sweep the area, finding that the bunkers were built at ground level. This is how the VC caused the death of two men and the wounds to many others. That, and their ability to keep the company pinned down by this type of gun fighting.

Many VC bodies, said Joe G. and others, were found after the artillery shelling stopped. They completed the sweeping of the area before the choppers returned. They then medic-vacced the dead and wounded back to Cu-Chi on these helicopters, and the choppers flew the company back to its field base camp.

Because of other activity in many of the other areas, our company went on many eagle flights, we encountered small battles with the VC. None compared to the Cambodian border, thank God.

XII

The Return to the Cambodian Border

When we left Tri-Nung we went to Providence to help guard the bunker line. We arrived by convoy to Providence. Captain Coronet was the company C.O. We only stayed in Providence to guard the bunker line for two days. It may have had something to do with the way the armor unit patrolled and pulled their guard duty at night.

These guys would fire their M–60 machine guns at anything, and there would be nothing out there to even shoot at, which made it too hard to sleep at night. For the first time ever I would have rather been in the field than with these crazy guys. That may have been the reason that these units are overrun more than the foot soldiers; they were too noisy.

The company set up a field base camp site outside of Providence and the Brothers built another "Soul Bunker." It had to be taken down, because the Colonel needed the PSP and sand bags for his bunker. They told us to give this material to the Colonel.

With much reluctance the Colonel received the material. After we had set up the inside and outside parameter we started reconning the area daily, where there were pungee pits and many other tree-type and ground-type booby traps used by the VC.

After many days of carrying the radio, my back began hurting a great deal. The next day I went on the convoy to see the doctor and he gave me some pills and a note for rest. As part of my rest I had latrine duty. That meant I had to burn human waste, with diesel fuel, and then bury it after most of the waste had burned away. I had this latrine duty for four days; that's how long the note from the doctor said I needed rest for my back.

We also received a new Lieutenant in the company. I met him that day just after I had taken my pills for my back. They had made me groggy, so as I was speaking to the Lieutenant, I slipped. The Lieutenant told me that he could write me up for being on drugs. I told him that I was not on drugs, just that I was a little groggy from the medication that the doctor had given me.

He did not believe me and was going to take me to the Captain. I told him that I was leaving. His M–16 was taken apart and left on top of the bunker. He was cleaning it. He said, If you don't stop I'll shoot you. Then I stopped and turned. I walked back three steps and stood face-to-face with the Lieutenant and said, Before you can get your M–16, I'll cut your throat. You're in Nam now Lieutenant, not in the States. Then I turned and walked away. The Lieutenant went and told the Captain. The Captain walked over to my bunker and said, I heard you met the new Lieutenant. I said I did. The Captain then said, He wants to have you court martialed for threatening an officer. I said, He does? Well, Captain, what are you going to do?

The Captain answered, well Two-Four, if we were in the States, I would court martial you. I said, The Lieutenant said that if I did not stop walking he was going to shoot me. Shoot you where? the Captain asked. I guess in my back, so I turned and walked back to him and told him that I'd cut his throat before he could get his M–16.

Then the Captain called the Lieutenant and asked him, why he wanted to shoot me. The Lieutenant said, Because I told him to stop. The Captain said, What order did he disobey? None sir, the Lieutenant replied. The Captain turned and said, I'm sorry about this Two-Four, and walked away, leaving the Lieutenant standing there. The lieutenant said, I should not have said I was going to shoot you. I'm sorry. I said, You're new and you have a lot to learn. Welcome to the 2nd Battalion Wolfhounds.

Two days later Indian and I went on an LP patrol 200 feet from the front gate. We had done stupid things; it would have been better to stand up and be sacrificed to Sir Charles than lay down in the open area.

The odds of Indian and me making it back alive to the parameter, if Sir Charles came, would have been none. If we were not killed by Sir Charles, the guys on the bunker line in our parameter would have shot us as we ran for the front gate. Indian and I were two dead men.

We had two-hour shifts in rotation for pulling guard duty as the other person tried to sleep. Indian got really comfortable out there and started snoring. I woke him up, but he was a little irate when I did that. So I told him that if he didn't stop snoring I'd cut his throat.

We remained on the patrol until seven o'clock the next morning. Later that day I told the Captain I wanted out of the field. I told him that I was scared that these guys were going to sleep on guard duty and snore like they're at home in their bed. That's nerve racking.

The Captain replied, As long as you're afraid, I know you'll shoot and that's what we need; men that are afraid. Now, if you told me that you were not afraid, then I would need to remove you from the field, because you may be in shock. That's dangerous to the unit. I said, I'm not afraid. Then Ed, Joe G., the Captain, and I just laughed.

The next day the whole company was on patrol. The Captain gave orders to move out and that we were heading southwest, but the new Lieutenant told me to go north. So I said, We are supposed to go southwest, not north. He said, I gave you an order, Private. I answered, Sir I'm not a private, I'm a corporal. Just then the Captain walked up and said, What's the hold up, Two-Four? The Lieutenant said, I gave this Private or whatever his rank is an order to go north and he refused to do so. Then the Captain turned to me and asked, Two-Four what direction were we heading in? I said, Southwest. He said, Let's move out.

Then the Lieutenant said, Captain that's wrong, we should be going north. The Captain said, Lieutenant you're new so I'm not going to bust you, but if you keep beating up on Two-Four you will be. The Captain said, I gave Two-Four orders to go southwest. He knows what he is doing, he can read the maps better than our officers, so get in the ranks before you're left out here to deal with Sir Charles by yourself. The other guys laughed quickly, then they stopped.

We then moved out southwest to set up our ambush location for that night. The Lieutenant apologized to me the next morning after we had returned to our field base camp and he had had an opportunity to review the map of our ambush location. He was a nice guy after he stopped pushing his rank around and decided to live and stop trying to be a hero.

This had been the longest place we had stayed in, for almost two months, but there was talk about the Wolfhounds returning to the Cambodian border. The difference this time was that the whole 2nd Battalion of the Wolfhounds would engage in the battle on the Cambodian border.

We would have bunkers, barbed wire, RPG screens, and more of everything for protection, which we did not have the two other times we were on the Cambodian border. Charlie company would not be with us, they were on another mission near the border, about ten clicks away.

So Alpha company was leaving the Tri-Dong area for a one-night stand down before going to the border, in Providence. We left by convoy that day. We were still in the Tet-Offensives, from the Viet Cong; this was one of the reasons there were many little battles all over Vietnam.

The commander of the 25th Division wanted Alpha company on the border, because of the fantastic job they said we had done defeating the VC. That night, most of the guys drank beer. I had soda and we went over to the Wolfhounds club, where a few guys had a Wolfhound drink.

This drink was a mixture of one shot of everything on the bar. Paul took a few steps after his Wolfhounds drink and began to fall. We caught him and took him outside in time. He then threw up everything; he was one sick Wolfhound.

Ed and I returned to the barracks for rest, to battle the regular VC army on the Cambodian border. As I laid down that night I could not forget about Sergeant Williams, even though he was killed trying to save Peter, and how he moved so smoothly, like a matador, when he was charged by the water buffalo trying to keep us from becoming injured by this beast.

Also, he protected the village people by doing this matador act; otherwise, the water buffalo would have been killed, for charging us. That would have upset the people in the village, because the water buffalo was their means of transportation, along with their plow horses.

The next day the hornet helicopter pilots flew in the Battalion area to fly us to the Cambodian border. The helicopter gun ships were ready and waiting to prep the landing area, with rockets, M–79, M–60, WP, and M–16 gunfire. The Shounook helicopter would bring all the supplies needed to build bunkers, food, barbed wire, more claymore mines, trip flares, mortar rounds, M–90 Bazooka bee-hive rounds, and radio equipment. Major Skonion would fly out later, once the parameter was secured by 2nd Battalion.

The Tet-Offensive was a united effort by the VC under the leadership of Ho-Chi-Minh, to defeat the American and Australian armies. Entering the southern part of Vietnam in every spot or location possible, with the northern entries at the same time, was designed to confuse the Americans and make them think that they were being attacked from every corner, and every angle. This left one to think that the North Viet Cong had invaded South Vietnam. We would not have a chance to make it out alive, let's run for our lives.

It was psychology, but it kept the American and Australian soldiers off balance, because of the waves of VC soldiers attacking the American and Australian parameters all at once. The only thing that a person could envision is being overrun and froze, seeing this many soldiers charging towards them at once.

That's how the VC had become victorious in many of their battles, until the first time they met the Wolfhounds 2nd Battalion Alpha company. Alpha company made a stand and received rear support from the helicopter gunners. We wanted to live; our inner strength, and God, could create the abilities of survival to defeat the enemies if you have faith in Him.

Now, with the two other companies and the additional protection Alpha company had to instruct the other companies on, what was expected on the Cambodian border? The divisions up north had it bad. Charlie and Delta company of our Division (25th), went up North to help the 4th Calvary unit and the 101 Airborne unit. They said it was a rough fire fight, in the rubber tree plantation.

The 25th Division was located in the Southern part of Vietnam. We received more rain than they did in the Northern part of Vietnam, but were not better off, because the activity was shifting to the south, so the VC could close the back door on the Americans and Australians to gain their victory as the VC moved up north from the south.

This is why it was so important for the 25th Division to stop the VC from crossing the Cambodian border; so they would not be able to defeat the American and Australian armies. We had to stop this movement to the north. This was a tall order that the 25th Division had to handle.

The Americans were in Vietnam initially to discover other minerals (tin, rubber, oil, etc.) to help the United States's economy and also to supply U.S. troops to help the Australian army up north.

The communist government had kicked France out and France asked Australia to help. France then pulled out, leaving Australia to help the Vietnamese people to fight the Communist party in North Vietnam.

Because of the American civilians that lost their lives, Australia then asked the United States for soldiers, supplies, and money, which was granted. We were in for a long haul: from 1958-1975, the longest war ever for the Americans.

After we landed, six clicks from the border, we began sweeping the area, up to a location that would become our Battalion camp parameter and battle ground. Delta company continued, with their sweep of the area one click beyond the selected battalion camp parameter and set up guard locations, while the 2nd, 3rd, and engineering platoons strung barbed wire, set up trip flares, and built bunkers for everyone.

Ed, Miller, Joe G., and I built Major Skonion bunker, our Captain's bunker, and the CP's bunker. It normally gets dark a little after 9:00 P.M. as it does in the U.S. during the summer in Connecticut. It was about 4:00 that afternoon and three of the bunker areas assigned to our platoon had not been built yet. But the Captains for the three companies (Alpha, Bravo, and Delta) plus the Major's bunkers were completed. They were safe and comfortable in their bunkers that we had just built.

Around 4:00 P.M., Delta company returned to the parameter only to find that the bunkers they needed for protection had not been built. So Lieutenant Nebask wanted me and two other guys to build his bunker. I said no, then I said okay, but don't come to our bunker once the fighting begins, because I'll kick you out if you do.

I told the Lieutenant that, because he was so afraid that he only thought of himself, no one else mattered. We all were afraid, but the guys worked together to provide protection, as quickly as possible and not just standing around to give orders.

The other Lieutenants filled sand bags and help build their platoon bunkers, but not Lieutenant Nebask. He was afraid he would not survive his six months in the field. If he did, he would be removed from the field in April of 1969. This was the month of February 1969, and the worst thing was, that we were on the Cambodian border.

We finally completed building the Lieutenant's bunker and were very tired, but had to build our bunker before the VC attacked us later that night. It was around seven o'clock. Ed and Yates had already started building our bunker. Each bunker on the front line had to be large enough for five to six men to fit in and be able to fire their weapons from within the bunker.

Each bunker had a back splash wall to provide added protection from VC RPG rockets or mortar round scrapped metal fragments. It must have been around 9:30 P.M. when we laid the last sand bag. We then ate our C-rations and laid on top of the bunker, looking at the clear night sky that had a full moon.

We were able to catch our breath, as we sat, not having the need to fill any more sand bags or do anything else, but wait on the VC.

They were going to send out two LP patrols, one from Delta, the other from Bravo company. I said, Are they crazy? The Captain said, This is what the Major wanted. I said, The Major wanted to have lives lost just to save his? The Captain said, Well Two-Four, the Major is calling the shots.

The Captain left, as the two companies were seeing their LP squads out of the camp parameter gate. Ed, Yates, Rick, Joe G., Paul, and I noticed the mortar and artillery unit behind our bunker, about 200 feet back. But we had made our splash wall two sand bags wide and thick; a wall that was about seven feet long and four feet high.

This was the first week in February 1969; the time of the month when the moon shines the brightest. We remained outside of the bunker to enjoy the nice cool breeze, as we all kind of closed our eyes for a minute or two. For the most part we talked all night long.

Around 1:30 A.M. we heard, Thumb! Thumb! Thumb! It was incoming rounds, mortars rounds and rockets launched by the Viet Cong into our parameter. We quickly moved our tired bodies off from the top of the bunker to the inside of our bunker to take our fighting position.

We then heard screams over the radio from one of the LP patrols that had been overrun by the VC. The VC had wounded each man. Some injuries were more serious than others, but Sir Charles told them they would be back to finish them off after they had overtaken the Battalion camp parameter.

Our Battalion camp parameter was a circle. The VC's

151

three Battalions moved into attacking from all sides of the parameter. They were determined to take our parameter, killing us in the process, but the Wolfhounds had the same determination to keep the VC out of the parameter, killing them as they approached the barbed wire fence.

Sir Charles launched an RPG rocket. It was directed at our bunker. Thank God for the RPG screen that we put up; it intersected the rocket, exploding it into pieces twenty-five feet in front of our bunker.

There was just part of an RPG screen left that would still provide some protection. Ed was firing his M–60, while the rest of us fired our M–16; our bunker was in direct line of the border.

The artillery unit lowered their barrel and began firing bee-hive rounds over the bunker, killing the VC as they charged our bunker. The artillery unit fired fifteen bee-hive rounds over our bunker. They did not see any movement from our bunker so they assumed we were all killed from the RPG round.

Otherwise, the artillery unit would not have fired any bee-hive rounds over our bunker at all. Even though the VC had picked up the barbed wire and was running toward us with it, it was frightening. We continued firing our weapons, dropping as many of the VCs, as they charged our bunkers.

That's when the artillery unit started shooting their bee-hive rounds over our bunker, to save themselves. We were assumed dead. Lieutenant Nebask, ran over to our bunker. When I saw him enter, I stopped firing my weapon and pushed him out of the bunker opening. He was then hit by a piece of scrapped metal in the back.

He then crawled back to his bunker. I looked out of one of our firing portholes and noticed that his bunker was hit by an RPG rocket, which flattened the bunker. From the weight of the bunker on the guys on the inside, some were injured.

The Lieutenant ran and left those injured under the collapsed bunker; he then returned to help those that were injured at his bunker after I had pushed him out of our bunker.

After Ed, Joe G., Willie, Yates, Rick, Paul, and I stepped out of the bunker, which surprised the artillery unit, they shouted hooray, after noticing that we were not dead; if not from the RPG rocket, then from their fifteen bee-hive rounds shot over our bunker.

We then looked at the sand bags, used as our splashed wall, and saw little pin holes in these bags of sand, as some of the dirt slowly drained out of the bags. Ed, Yates, Willie, Rick, Paul, and Joe G. cursed and then they said, thank God! I thanked God! I just thank God. That's all.

God had given us strength to go on to build this bunker. Its fortification withstood that battle. We all just thanked God again and again as tears formed in my eyes. We knew without the splash wall that our own artillery unit would have killed us, for sure.

It was a frightening experience seeing a wave of men running at you, and none appear to have been hit from your bullets. No one was falling, or they just did not fall fast enough from our gunfire.

They were charging our bunker. All you saw was death and you had no way to stop it. I was firing my M–16 so fast that the barrel was too hot to hold. The next morning we saddled up to get a body count. This time there were more dead bodies; still, many had been taken back across the border.

The medics went out to the LP patrols to take care of the wounded, to prepare them to be medi-vacced back to Cu-Chi's hospital.

The next day we walked through the canals. Joe G. and Peewee were not tall enough to walk through the canal. So I put Joe G. on my back and Miller placed Peewee on his back. Both Joe G. and Peewee looked out, as we crossed this canal, to make sure that Sir Charles was not present as we moved to the other side.

The place that we crossed in the canal had a hard bottom, plus the water was clear, but up to my chin. This hard bottom made it somewhat easier for us to carry additional weight and we did not sink into the mud. As we walked across the canal, we were like sitting ducks, because of the height of the water.

You would have had to understand, "The Lord is my Shepherd" the Bible verse, to know that I prayed each step that I took; as well as for others not to step on any mines under the water, as we moved across to the other side.

That distance across the canal was a hundred yards. Miller and I carried Joe G. and Peewee that distance to safety. Everyone was wet; Joe G. and Peewee were wet from the waist down. It was a hot day, like always, so within a few hours everyone was dry, but we still had water in our boots that was pumped out through the air holes on the arches of the boots as we continued our march through the jungle.

We continued our search for the VC after having this heavy battle earlier this morning with him. We must have gone two clicks away from our Battalion camp parameter, according to the map, as we checked our grid core (latitude and longitude) location.

As we continued our sweep of the area, we had to cross another canal. We did not want to swim across, so two men quickly swam across the canal to get the sand pan (a boat) as the rest of the platoon provided gun coverage for them against Sir Charles, should he happen to be nearby.

Once the two guys returned with the sand pan, some of the other guys got in to set up guards, on the other side until the whole platoon had made it to that other side. This area had thick hedged rolls and we wanted to be sure that, if the VC had set an ambush for us, that one man would not engage in a gunfight by himself.

Leeches were most likely in this canal. We identified that by the dirty-looking, thick of the water. The movement the first two guys made to the water alerted the leeches that there was life nearby that they could cling to our bodies to suck your blood.

Three other guys got into the sand pan once it returned to the platoon where we were waiting to go over on the other side. They then went to the other side, where the one guy was left to watch out for the VCs.

Then once the sand pan returned for the second time three of us guys got in to cross the canal. Once we had reached the other side, each man got up and was helped out of the sand pan.

Well, the guy before me was getting ready to get out. He slipped off the bank and his foot kicked the sand pan, which caused the sand pan to rock. Because I stood up with the radio on my back it threw me off balance, which forced me overboard.

It all happened so quickly. I quickly dropped my helmet, M–16, and ammo inside of the sand pan, as it threw me out of the sand pan. I went down and under in the canal, with sixty pounds on my back, but by the grace of God, the radio acted like a life jacket and popped me up to the surface of the water.

Everyone said they turned and you were no longer in the sand pan; then we blinked and there you were, on the left side of the sand pan.

The guys pulled me out of the water and noticed that I

was not wet from my shoulders to my waist. I then had a different appreciation for the radio (pick-25), more than what I had had before. After this event we cautioned everyone how to get out of the sand pan, and then completed the canal crossing.

The area that was crossed over into the sand pan, became our LP site for that night. We set up an ambush area against the VCs, because we had been told that the VCs used this canal for transporting supplies to their troops.

We had to radio the Captain to inform him that we had found no additional bodies and let them know our grid core in case we needed artillery support. Then the Captain said that we should stay at this location to stop the VC.

There was no activity that night on the canal, but it was not a good set up site; about 100 feet away from the bank of the canal. I wondered what type of defense we would have had against the VC with all of these trees.

Sir Charles could use an RPG rocket, that would hit the trees and kill or wound many of us, because we had no protection or cover at all. We were out in the open, behind some trees. This was real jungle action. Ready or not, we all felt numb and we all worried about the shot we wouldn't hear, that could kill us.

The next morning we contacted our company CP and the Captain informed us to continue looking for the VC. We wanted to reverse this psychological process that the VC had placed on us, by hunting him like he was a beast. With this type of momentum by our unit, Sir Charles would not have time to re-group and rebuild his forces, as fast as he would have liked.

You see the Viet Cong lived underground, hospitals or other living quarters underground.

When we found tunnels, we would send the smallest

guy that wanted to play hero in the tunnels. He would take two .45 pistols with him, but first we would throw one or two grenades in the tunnel before this guy went in. Sometimes, he would find something; most of the time he would find nothing.

The VC would also hang snakes at the entrances of the tunnels, like a viper snake. One bite, you're dead; this snake blends right in with the terrain, which would make it very difficult to detect. Once the grenade had exploded, it might have killed this snake or VC near the entrance of the tunnel.

As we continued sweeping the area on the border, we were unable to find any sign of the VC; that meant no activity. Our search returned us back to the Battalion camp parameter, where Bravo company then went on a recon of the area. They also had made plans to set up their LP patrol area later that night.

We remained on the Cambodian border for four days; then we were told by the Captain that we had to dismantle the bunkers and return to our prior field base camp locations. That's what the Colonel told the Captains from all three companies.

The fourth day arrived. On that morning the Battalion's three companies (Alpha, Bravo, and Delta) removed and emptied the sand bags. PSP (a flat metal which can be used for the roof of the bunkers, where some sand bags are placed), barbed wire, claymore mines, trip flares, RPG screens, etc., that would be picked up by the shounook helicopter.

The three companies then started on their way to return to their prior camp parameter on foot. Most of the individual camps for each company was eight to ten miles from the Battalion camp located on the Cambodian border.

On our way we noticed signs that said, "Tu-die (meaning kill zone)"; that meant it was booby trapped, or there might be an ambush ahead. We did notice a mortar round that did not explode when it was fired, so the demo man placed a charge of C-4 to blow this round away.

We could not leave the round stuck in the ground, because the VC would make a booby trap out of the round. It would kill other U.S. troops if they came in this area; they might trip over the wire and become wounded and dead men.

Scrapped metal from that mortar round, once it had exploded, zinged by my head. Whoop that was close.

This was a ten-mile sweep and the radio did not get any lighter as we continued our sweep. We finally arrived to the area. There was an armor unit on the other side in the Providence location. Sniper fire was received once we moved closer to this camp location.

The firing of the armor tank guns went on each day and night, I guess to keep Sir Charles away; but it did not help us, The Wolfhounds, feel better by being there with this armor unit in the Bang-Train area.

XIII

How Fast Are You Really?

The VC was shooting a machine gun at us as we were walking up this narrow path. Everyone hit the ground for cover. I fell and took cover on the right, the radio still on my back. Ed, Joe G., and everyone else were on the left. The point man was up further than I, but he was on the left side and unable to return gunfire to the VC.

The bullets from the VC machine gun quickly started down the path, allowing no one to move. We then realized that the VC was in a concealed spot, but he was able to keep us pinned down.

The machine gun fire increased over my body, because I had the radio. If the VC killed me, that meant the platoon could not radio for additional help. The VC then would be able to pick them off one by one; if anyone tried to get to the radio that was on my back, if I was dead.

Each time I moved just a little in any direction, a burst of machine gunfire would be shot in my direction. Being on the right side in this fighting position, on my back, I fired my M–16, at fully-automatic at the tree that was knocked down from artillery shelling, where the smoke came from after this VC stopped firing his machine gun.

I had tilted my head, with my helmet still on my head, as I viewed my rounds hitting the tree and the rounds going up towards the VC machine gun nest. Then the other guys were able to also return gunfire, but it was not enough. I then received a heavy burst of machine gunfire sprayed across my body.

I was nervous and upset, but continued firing from my back position, as best as I could. After Ed and Yates fired a few rounds, I was able to turn over, off my back. We all started laying some heavy gunfire in that VC direction.

I called Alpha 6, Alpha 6, this is Alpha 2 over, this is Alpha 6 over, Alpha 6 we are pinned down by a Victory Charlie, sniper machine gunfire; they are approximately one hundred-fifty meters in front of our position.

I gave Alpha 6 our grid cores and popped our purple smoke so the spotter helicopter could spot our smoke and tell the artillery unit where to fire their shells short of the one hundred and fifty meters. The artillery rounds landed right in the tree area where the VC machine gunfire was coming from.

I then radioed Alpha 6 to have them stop firing. When the artillery shelling stopped we were able to get up slowly, moving quickly in on the VC machine gun nest. We searched this area, and no VC. He had left the area, again!

After this two-hour delay we finally made it to our destination. This new area was closer to Cu-Chi than any other area we had set up in before. This location had the big guns and howitzers, but a weak bunker line, without barbed wire, claymore mines, and trip flares. Joe G., Willie, and I were walking up to our company CP and had to pass the artillery battery location on our way. The artillery unit started firing their howitzer as we were directly in the location of that area. The first two rounds that were fired frightened us. The pressure and force of the firing of the rounds had shook the earth, lifting us off of our feet into the air.

We landed on our backs as we fell to the ground, and found ourselves somewhat disoriented as to how we ended up on the ground. The artillery unit by then had fired eight more rounds, increasing our deafness and dizziness. They then stopped. Some of the guys, in the artillery unit noticed us on the ground and ran over to help Joe G., Willie, and me up off the ground.

Our legs gave way as we tried to stand up, so the men helped us to a nearby bunker wall, allowing us to collect ourselves from the artillery firing. The ringing remained for a few days afterwards, but it added to a problem in my hearing, from small weapons, that I am left with today.

We continued on to the CP, for C-rations and additional ammo. I was asked again, by one of the CP radio operators, if I wanted to be an RTO for the CP. I said no, I enjoyed being with these guys in my platoon, thank you for asking again. Then we left to return to our bunker.

The next day we went on a recon of the area, walking about five miles, then we returned to the parameter. Later that afternoon we went on an eagle flight, where we got off the choppers and below us was mud.

The choppers were about six feet in the air and everyone on the chopper jumped. Everyone that jumped off this chopper was knee high in mud but me. With the additional weight of the radio and my other gear, I sunk up to my waist in mud.

It looked like a death trap. No one could help the other get out of this mud. We were in the open, sitting ducks; the VC would have had a great day picking us off, as we ran for cover.

You see, I didn't have the problem of running for cover. I was stuck in the mud. I wanted, so much to live, but the mud was too hard for me to move my legs; it was like clay. So I removed my radio, then leaned forward, taking one leg out at a time. I couldn't walk on this mud; if I tried, I would have gotten sunk again.

The rest of the company provided cover for me as I struggled with this mud. I crawled on my stomach, drag-

161

ging my radio and M–16 for about 50 yards. I also thought about there being booby traps under this mud as I crawled on it. It took me an hour to crawl that distance.

This area we had landed in had been identified to be a cargo location on the canal, where the VC transported their supplies up and down the canal to other VC camps. Little did we know that the tide would rush in about ten o'clock that night, flooding the LP and our main locations.

I always kept a plastic bag with me to place the radio hand piece in, because of the rain and for crossing the canals. The Lieutenant had two guys from our platoon go down to a lower part, like a small island five feet in diameter, to set up as an LP patrol. This was done to give us early warning, if they saw the VC traveling on the canal.

I laid down on a rice patty dice (which is about 12 inches in width) and the other guys sat down in the rice field, resting themselves against the rice burn. Everyone tried to get as comfortable as possible for the night. I had the radio next to a bush to ensure it would remain dry, as I laid on my side on the rice dice.

During the night my arm reached out and my hand went down into the water. I lifted up my hand and body to see what the level of the water was in the rice field. The guys on the LP patrol were saying that the little island was covered by the water and it was still rising.

Just then the Lieutenant said, Come up here, but the water is rising up here also. So the guys returned to the little island, but the level of the water in our location was much lower than that on the little island used as the LP site.

Later the guys on the LP site changed their minds and wanted to come up top. They remained up top with the rest of our platoon until morning. Everyone that sat on the ground that night was chest-high in water.

The next morning myself and a couple of the other guys that were small enough to rest on the rice dice, were dry, but we had to cross the rice field where the rest of the platoon had slept that night. We all got wet crossing the rice field as we saddled up and moved out of the area.

After a lengthy recon of the area, the choppers returned to pick us up, bringing us back to Diamond IV, our new camp site. We just arrived there two days earlier. We had a day off to rest and clean up our weapons from the water and have some hot food.

A couple of days later we were again eagle flown to another area, where heavy VC activity had been reported. As we swept through the area it had started to rain, which was a problem, because it always rained six or seven times a day, but this day it rained into the night. The choppers are flown less during the time that it is raining, so we were going to spend the night out here in the rain.

It was dark and colder than normal as we spread out to watch for the VC to walk by our night ambush. We had planned to spring this ambush on the VC once they were detected.

I would have called this a storm, because of the downpour, known as a Monsoon in rainy season. The water collected at the top and rushed downward on the slope, overrunning the three-foot-high dices.

Some of the guys had ponchos; others just had ponchos liners and some guys had nothing at all. So much rain would cause your weapon to rust. So we poured LSA oil on the M–16, M–60, and our M–16 magazines. We had to be ready when Sir Charles came by; no rust, no rain, and fatigue would not stop us from being ready.

On top of everything else, this LP location was very scary. It was dark and the parameter provided very good cover for the VC, but not for us. We should have been in the hedger roll and not in the open area. You know, let's think a little.

We got up the next morning, wet, cold, angry, tired, hungry, and to some degree upset that we had been out there in this bad weather all night and didn't hear a bullet fired at all. We were also glad. Thank God for another day.

We then saddled up and started walking back to Diamond IV, where they had a hot breakfast waiting for us once we reconned and swept the area on our way back to Diamond IV. This was a sweep of about seven clicks before we walked through the front gates after having left at about 5:30 A.M. and arriving about 8:00 A.M.

The month of February 1969 was almost over, and it felt like I had been in Vietnam a lifetime. All I could hear in the mornings if we set up our LP patrol that night close to a village area was the music of this country and the sound of water buffaloes on the farm land.

I had made it through by the grace of God, with some major adjustments in my life, that had very little to do with my age or the color of my skin. God will make his decision as to what his will, will be for you.

Near the end of February, we were told that it might be possible the 2nd Battalion Wolfhounds would return to the Cambodian border. No one jumped for joy when the Lieutenant shared this information with the platoon.

The next day we went out on a night patrol LP. There was heavy, heavy VC activity in this area, where our LP patrol set up its ambush, but it rained all night again. I placed my radio on the rice dice behind me and everyone sat in the water up to their chest. After I sat on my helmet, which hurt, I then settled for sitting in the water, which was cold.

The water wasn't bad, after you had sat in it for a while, but once you were up, you got cold again when you stood up to pull guard duty. I said I didn't think Sir Charles would be that stupid to come out in all this rain; just us Americans, and we could end up sick behind this mission. We woke the next morning. I thanked God for this day. Then we looked at each other, as the water dropped from our pockets and off our clothes, with a smile. We said, Don't tell anyone in the States that we sat in the water all night waiting for Sir Charles; they will laugh at us.

And Sir Charles, he's in a dry bed maybe, with his women, and we are out here wet. It was sad in this place, but we were not playing war games, everything was for real. So we saddled up and reconned back to Diamond IV to have a hot breakfast once we made it through the front gates.

While we were at Diamond IV, there was a Vietnamese girl I had met. I spoke to her over the barbed wire fence. One day she brought some pictures of her family and showed them to me. She must have been about fifteen years old.

She would ask about me at the front gate, if she had not seen me every evening. I would give her some C-ration, if we had some extra, for her family, while I was stationed at Diamond IV.

Then we finally received the information for our company (Alpha) to return back to the border later that week. So we had to leave Diamond IV and return back to Cu-Chi to be eagle flown to the Cambodian border with other companies in our Battalion.

The next morning when we had prepared to leave Diamond IV, this girl rode her bicycle behind our truck. Then some of the Caucasian guys started throwing C-ration cans at her. I told them to stop. They stopped throwing the C-ration cans, then one guy said, Is she your girl friend? I said, No, she just a girl that's a friend of mine; she has not done anything to anyone, just stop throwing the C-ration cans. She yelled out to me, Joe I will miss you! I told her that I will miss her; she was a friend to me, someone different than talking to guys all the time.

The truck increased the distance between her bicycle as we went forward to Cu-Chi. The truck took us to Cu-Chi just before we went to our new location. The next day we eagle flew back to the Cambodian border, where we again built bunkers, then built our bunker just before the battle began later that night.

Once night had fallen the sergeant approached me and said, Two-Four you're going on the LP patrol tonight. I said, No I'm not. I continued talking: You know how dangerous it is on the border and you expect me to go outside of this parameter on some suicide mission, no way.

The sergeant said, You either go or I'll shoot you right here. I said, I can kill you also, so don't talk to me about shooting someone. You were up here and were wounded on that LP patrol, when we came to the border the first time. And now, this is your second time on the border and this would be my fourth time in three weeks altogether that I've spent on the border. I know what's out there. You may have forgotten, while you spent time recovering from your wounds, while I remained in the field. The sergeant turned away from me and then asked Hudson to go. I was not going to go. I said, You can court martial me, do whatever, I am not going to purposely get myself killed, to obey a stupid order by some Colonel so he could receive a battle metal.

So the sergeant placed me in a bunker on the other side of the Battalion parameter. Hudson, Peewee, Charles, and others from Delta and Alpha company went on this LP patrol; eleven men not knowing that this would be their last mission.

I tried to talk the sergeant into hiding the men on the bunker lines and faking the transmission to the CP and at the same time protecting the lives of these men. They had to go and see the Captain, the sergeant said, The Colonel feels it is important to have this early warning for the main parameter.

The eleven men saddled up and moved out of the parameter to their LP location around 9:45 P.M. They were on the west side of the parameter, about 150 meters away. After they were in their position they radioed the CP to let them know that they were at their location.

Around eleven-thirty that night I received a call from the LP patrol telling me that they had seen VC activity (movement) out in front of their location. I called our CP and spoke to the Captain, telling him that the LP have spotted movement. I stated that we have time to bring the men in from the LP patrol into the parameter before the VC attack.

The Captain then called the Colonel to ask permission to bring the men back in the parameter. The Colonel said, No! I told the Captain, with tears in my voice that the men are going to be killed if we don't bring then back in now. The Captain was angry with the Colonel's decision and said to me, Look, an order is an order, roger out!

All I could do was pray for the LP patrol that night that someone would make it back alive. I had to tell them that their request to come in the parameter was turned down and they had to remain on the LP patrol.

At about 1:00 A.M., the gun battle began. An RPG rocket hit the side of the hole that the LP patrol had set up in, killing three or four men. Peewee got on the horn, crying for help: We are being overrun! We are being overrun! Help, help. I tried talking to Peewee, but he said, Two-Four I know you tried. I have to go.

The battle was very intense and it was hard to hold the VC back. I guess Peewee, Hudson, and some of the other guys were killed running back to the parameter. They may have gotten caught between the VC gunfire and the Delta company, on the west side of the parameter gunfire, but they were dead.

Or maybe the Delta side of the parameter shot Peewee, Hudson, and the other guys, thinking that they were VC. Then the VC walked on the LP patrol as they have done in the past; only this time they killed the rest of the men on the LP patrol and not just wounded them.

The cry of death from the LP patrol was over. Sir Charles then moved quickly, with their three Battalions, to overrun our parameter. I looked out in front of my bunker; it looked like two hundred men at the first three rolls of barbed wire. You could hear something different in this battle than the others that we had been in on the border. This was a big battle.

We had learned from many battles to aim knee-high, to shoot our weapons just as Sir Charles did. The VC were at the wire. I continued firing my M–16 on semi-automatic. They were falling from each burst I released. I had no help but God, and was no longer too afraid to take aim and fire my weapon.

The Wolfhounds had reversed the battle in small weapon gun battles. But the more I killed, the more VC appeared in their place. I held my position to do battle, maybe because I knew deep down that the eleven men on the LP patrol were already dead.

This may have angered me to have frozen my thinking on killing Sir Charles. An RPG rocket then hit the bunker on my left. One guy managed to crawl out and over to my bunker to ask me for help, to get the other guys out.

The artillery unit fired a couple of bee-hive rounds,

between my bunker and the one that was hit and had fallen from the RPG round. Sir Charles was then down off the barbed wire and the other VC left this location. I was then able to help this guy from Delta company, with his friends that were in the bunker. After we had taken the guys out of the fallen bunker, I started back to my bunker by crawling low, the same way that I went over to help this guy.

I then stopped, because I heard the sound of scrapped metal whistling through the air. I didn't know where to go, having twenty feet to crawl before I would reach my bunker. I was still firing my M–16 at the VC that had not left the barbed wire. I moved back to my bunker as I listened to the scrapped metal ripping through the air and the bullets flying over my head. Something pinched the palm of my right hand.

I then moved my hand to look. The scrapped metal hit and killed this land crab. If I had not moved my hand this three-inch piece of metal would have gone through my hand, or worse, if I had moved five inches to the right it would have hit me in the head or back and killed me.

Sometimes it is hard to understand the sacrifices that are made on your behalf that will keep you and others alive. The grace of God. I then made it back to my bunker, grabbing some more M–16 magazines, and continued firing at the VC.

The wounded VC were unable to help or be helped by their fellow man to carry him off as they have done in so many of their battles. This was a do or die mission for the VC and the Wolfhounds. Many of the problems, this time, for the VC were that when they went to help the wounded, they were also wounded. Again it was a different type of battle for us this time.

It has always frightened the American soldier to see hundreds of VC charging at once. To kill him, the psychology of this approach by the VC, would add confusion to your mind, forcing you to do anything other than defend yourself with the fire power you had.

This often brought on sweat, tears, shell-shock, and nervousness. This war we did not want to win, politics, it would have too many financial strings attached; if we had won, more so than what we provided as aid to Vietnam, now.

The next morning we were told the sad news from the first sergeant, about the men who were on the LP patrol. They were all killed, he said. I told him that we had trip flares to go off, when someone crossed that area. Why was it necessary to lose these eleven lives. The first sergeant did not say, anything, but turned and walked away.

The first sergeant returned to our area to select men for a burial detail of the VC bodies. I was selected to be part of this burial team. The other men were selected to guard us against VC snipers and the possibility that a VC might be just wounded, but not dead. Because of the heat, the bodies would begin to smell very quickly. We had to be careful, because the Viet Cong has been known to pull the grenade pin and rest their bodies on it as they were taking their last breath of life. So, when the body is rolled over, the grenade handle will be released allowing the grenade to explode and kill the American soldier. As we walked out of our parameter, there were many Viet Cong bodies around the parameter and there were deep holes that had been made by our bulldozer for the burial.

Once I made it to the first VC body, I wrapped the ropes around his legs, then started pulling him into the hole. I heard this groaning sound. I stopped and dropped the ropes. I didn't have a weapon, just a gas mask. I started to run. Then I stopped, and noticed that it was the sound one made when a dead body is moved.

I pulled him in the hole and returned many more times placing the Viet Cong bodies on top of each other in this hole which would be covered by our bulldozer once we had removed all the bodies that were outside of our battle Battalion parameter. The other body that I pulled, I heard a pop, and the two other guys said Run, this body has a grenade under it. But it did not explode. We had our demo man come out to blow the grenade, with some C–4 charge to explode it inside of that hole.

On the other side of the parameter a VC was playing dead, but was wounded and was going to shoot the guy that was pulling his body in the hole. The guard saw the VC pull his gun, and the guard shot and killed the VC.

It was hot and the day was longer because of this detail and now the VC were trying to play dead, booby trap bodies and we were unsure if we were going to make it off the border alive after this battle. I was sure that Sir Charles would be back with even more troops than there were early this morning. We finally finished this detail to return back inside the parameter.

We had played a dangerous game, fighting a war that we did not win. We lost all those lives and had many men return home wounded, in mind or body or both. We never had a front line. Your front line was where you placed your barbed wire, claymore mines, trap flares and bunkers, for that time, and that time only.

There wasn't a front line as it was known to be, like in World War I and II and the Korean War. This war did not assign the infantry soldier to a designated position to guard until their tour of duty was up. Oh no. We went on a hunting trips, stalling the Viet Cong, big and bad American soldiers.

Well, we remained on the Cambodian border for about three more days to recon the area, but found nothing; only more VC dead bodies one or two miles from our battle Battalion parameter.

I asked Joe G. what he was going to tell Hudson's family. Joe G. was writing Hudson's sister and Joe G. didn't know what to say. All eleven American bodies had been flown back to Cu-Chi to be shipped home to their parents or wives.

Many times I thank God for standing in front of me, when I told the sergeant, No. I knew it was not me, but God, that kept me in the parameter that night and with every action of safety that I have taken while in Vietnam.

After the third day we took down the bunkers, barbed wire, PSP, claymore mines, and trip flares and sent them back to Cu-Chi on the Shounook helicopter. Our company returned to Providence base camp for a stand down from the battle field. New clothes and showers were available once we arrived in Providence base camp. That night they had two movies to show us; a stag movie and a John Wayne movie called Green Barge.

They changed the stag movie and put the John Wayne movie on. I got up and walked out of the door, on my way to my barracks. We remained in the Providence area to go on overnight missions and daytime recon sweeps. March was not a bad month. Nothing great happened; we just maintained ourselves, but the officers were moving out and onto different things.

In the month of April 1969, we received a new Captain. Captain Coronet's tour of duty (six months) was now over and he went into Cu-Chi to relax for six months before returning to the United States. Lieutenant Nebask also returned to Cu-Chi; his six months in the field were up. Doc, the medic, had two more months left in the field, because the medic did six to eight months of field duty.

Us, poor grunts, the soldiers that got pushed around

had to do the twelve months unless something happened. Our only way out of the field sooner than twelve months was to be badly wounded or killed.

They felt that the medic had seen too much blood. The Lieutenants and Captains had too much stress and too much responsibility, because of the men's lives they had in their hands. That's why they had less time in the field than the enlisted men.

We were still stationed in the Providence area, but our new assignment was to reduce the number of VC rockets launched into Providence. This was the same problem they had when we first came up to Providence months ago, but we were requested to go to another area.

Many bamboo trees were cut down to be used for the launching of the VC rockets. So we had to find the location that they were using to launch their rockets. We arrived by helicopter that next morning to recon and sweep the area. We finally located the bamboo that had been used for the launching of their rockets.

We then destroyed them, and moved about three hundred meters from that launching location to build our bunkers, setting up a parameter within this area to catch the VC before he launched more rockets into Providence.

We were putting our final touches to the building of our bunkers, when rockets were launched at our parameter. The first rocket exploded after hitting the tree tops one hundred feet behind our bunker.

I looked up as the scrapped metal fragments fell to the ground after the rocket exploded over the bunker that was near the trees. I said to myself, Surely some of the men assigned to that bunker must have gotten injured from the rocket scrapped metal.

I thought that as I entered our bunker, Not one of us had taken his weapon from off or from the side of our bunker, to bring it inside with him. The rockets shot by the VCs were walking inside the parameter, as the VC fired them behind us, hitting our CP and killing a Sergeant, Lieutenant, Captain, and a radio operator.

We had just received the new Captain and Lieutenant. Now they were gone; this war took everything from you. Tears began to come very hard for me, on the outside, but in the inside I cried always, for us all. I can smell the gun powder from the rockets. We never fired a round from our M–16; however, our mortar platoon had started firing mortar rounds were they, had seen flashes that could have been where the rockets where being launched.

We had to call the medic-vac chopper that night to take the wounded and dead to Providence base camp. The next morning one of the other CP radio operators asked me again if I wanted to be a radio operator in the CP. I said, Thank you, but no thank you.

After we started our sweep of the area and found nothing, that evening would be a repeat of last night's rocket fire launched in our parameter. Then we had artillery and the mortar platoon return rounds in the area that was identified to be the launching site of the rockets.

Firing back with mortars and artillery rounds stopped the VC from launching rockets at us for a while. The next day Alpha company had an overnight mission, so Charlie company took over this parameter in our place. Ed and I thought that we would see Madlock, because Charlie company was his company, but one guy told us that he went into Cu-Chi to see the doctor about something.

We swept the area and spoke to many of the people in the village about the VC activities and the people did say that they heard the VC each night as they came into the area. The mama-san pointed to where she had heard the VC voices.

That night Alpha company set up their LP site, about three hundred meters from the hooch in the village where we had spoken to the people. That night we looked out in front of us and saw someone with a claymore mine in their hands, viewing them through the star-light-scope. So we looked again through the star-light-scope and then identified him as being Robert, the school teacher.

Robert was sent back to the field after the eleven men were killed on the border. Robert had the detonator of the claymore mine in his hands as he sat next to the claymore mine.

Yates crawled out to where Robert was and told him to leave the claymore mine in the ground and return to the parameter, with the detonator only. We needed to spend more time with Robert, to help him to understand what was going on out in the field so he would not injure one of us or himself.

As the night went on, it became my turn to pull guard duty. I heard the VC talking to the Vietnamese lady in the hooch that had told us she would hear the VC at night. They were beating her to talk, so she would tell the VC which way we went. Maybe she said, she did not know, they just did not believe her so they kept hitting her.

I could not fire my weapon because I didn't know how many VC were in the area. When I woke up the next guy to pull guard duty, I told him about the VC hitting the lady in the hooch, and that he should make sure he is watching the VC so they will not walk upon us.

The hour was almost up for this guy to wake up the next guy to pull guard duty. This guy, an American Indian, was pulling guard. Then he noticed that a VC was standing about twenty feet in front of our parameter. He was so afraid, he didn't fire his weapon, but he instead jumped down on the ground so he would not be noticed by the VC.

He then crawled over to me and said, The VC is right in front of us. Sharp, a Brother, moved his M–16 magazines. This noise made the VC open fire on us with his weapon. I pulled my weapon up and fired as quickly as I possibly could. I then got up to get a medic for Sharp. I ran to the other side where our medic was, to inform him that Sharp was wounded.

At first by my running over to the medic they thought that I had been wounded. They wanted to hole me, and not allow me to return back to my position in the LP parameter. I told them that Sharp was shot in both of his wrists; he had received a million dollar wound. The medic went over and wrapped Sharp's wrists wounds. He would be on his way home after leaving the Cu-Chi hospital in Vietnam. But we first had to make it through this night.

Sharp had to wait until morning to be medic-vacced to the Providence hospital and later transfered to the Cu-Chi hospital. That morning as we secured the outside of the LP parameter before the medic-vac chopper arrived, we noticed some papers that were thrown on the ground between the two location spots, twenty feet from each location spot.

The VC were there. Maybe in another second or two they would have pushed their way through the hedged roll. I believe this because I opened fire, then everyone else did too. It made the VC run off, with the understanding that they may have been out numbered.

The medic-vac chopper finally arrived to pick up Sharp. We just looked at him as he flew away in the chopper. Sharp was the only one injured on the mission and was in the field for about two months. Now he was on his way home to the United States, after leaving the hospital. We then returned to a new location outside of the Cu-Chi area. Upon our arrival we were told that we had a new Lieutenant, who was an African-American. The new Lieutenant shared with us that he had been to Vietnam earlier as a Sergeant and requested reassignment to Vietnam again. I could not understand why he wanted Vietnam again, was it for money, or a vendetta with Sir Charles?

We went on many night LP patrols, but never had any action from the VC to fight them at any of the ambush locations. Time was also getting short for Ed and me and more caution was being used as we grew shorter in our time, left in Vietnam.

Over the next few days we received larger numbers of new guys added to our company and platoon. I was sick with some type of rash that required me to remain in the field base camp parameter, but took some time to tell the new guys what they should not do in the field.

Some of these guys just laughed, so I looked at them turned, and walked away, with a smile on my face. The next day the new guys went out on their first mission, with the entire company.

I was told after the company returned to the field base camp parameter, that one of the new guys saw a cigarette lighter hanging in a tree, and he pulled it which set the charge off that exploded the booby trap. The scrapped metal wounded and killed some men. The two new guys, a Lieutenant, and the radio operator were killed from the explosion, one incident which I tried to warn the new guys about.

The Captain was wounded, but he was more upset about the new guys going after the cigarette lighter. He said that he did not want this to happen again, and stated that he wanted more senior men in the field when he was going out on mission.

XIV

The Silence of Death, Without Warning a Friend

The company had returned very quickly from this mission after having the seriously injured, that were wounded, and the dead medic-vacced back to Cu-Chi.

A few days later our platoon went on another mission by eagle flight. We got off the choppers quickly and went for cover. I was walking point that day. I saw the trip wire to a booby trap after I had stepped over it, with one leg. I then called out to the rest of the platoon, Watch your step, there's a booby trap right here.

I guess a few guys heard me, but did not pass the word to all of the other guys. Meatball's foot came down on the trip wire. The booby trap exploded and scrapped metal fragments flew everywhere. Doc Brown was hit by a small piece in the stomach, and another piece in his back. Ed was hit in his hand and also caught a piece in the stomach.

I was standing closer to Meatball. When the booby trap exploded, Meatball was hit in the chest and died instantly. The chopper was no higher than fifty feet off the ground when this booby trap exploded. We immediately radioed for the chopper to come down to take Meatball in and any of the seriously wounded.

Meatball was dead, but we rushed him over to the chopper anyway, I guess because we felt that the doctors possibly could start his heart pumping again if he could get to the hospital.

Then this other guy was more afraid than anything else, so he got on, because he had been hit by a piece of scrapped metal in the back; a flesh wound just like the wound Ed and Doc Brown received. Doc, Willie, Ed, and I picked out the scrapped metal fragments from our bodies; we were hit, too. We just thanked God that our wounds were not really serious.

Thin area had many tunnels, so we would have our tunnel rat guy crawl in to find out what was going on. He received two .45 pistols and a grenade to place in the tunnel first; then he would enter. We found nothing in the tunnels and there wasn't any activity during this day.

On our mission everyone had two canteens of water, but most of the guys drank much too much water for a hot day like this one. We also had to remain out here overnight. Since this was a mission, with a number of days attached, I drank very little water, so my water would last me a longer period of time. We set up our night position inside of the hedger roll, which gave us some protection from Sir Charles.

The next morning many of the guys had drank all of their water, but I still had one and a half canteens of water left. We then wanted to find some water for everyone, because I shared my water with anyone of the men that needed something to drink. I did not have a Caucasian and African-American canteen. I just had a canteen and everybody drank from the same canteen, if they wanted some of my water.

There was an open field not far from our LP location; on the other side of the open field was a village. We had to cross this dried-out rice field to enter the village to get some water. We crossed this area one by one into the village, setting up our guard station as each man poured water into his canteen from the well.

We had been issued iodine tablets for this purpose (to drink bad water, using the iodine tablets to keep the water from making us too sick), but never had to use them before now. We placed the tablets into our canteens that had this dirty water in them. Because I shared my water with the whole platoon, that meant now I needed some of this unclean water. Some of this cloudy, buggy, diseased-looking water, was not bad, when you had no water.

I had just got one canteen full and dropped three iodine tables into the canteen of water. I gave it a couple of shakes to help the tables dissolve before I drank it. We were told by our CP that they wanted us to extend our mission for another day. They would drop us some C-ration so that our stomachs would have some food in them, to go along with this iodine, dirty, cloudy, buggy, diseased-looking water. That's just great. What else?

In the same area that we had eaten our C-ration in, dropped by the helicopter, we set up our night patrol. It was one hundred yards away from the village. We set up the trap flares and our claymore mines, but no barbed wire. We just waited for Sir Charles to come our way to ambush him.

It was a peaceful night. We looked at the sky and saw the stars as we felt the breeze of cool air blowing after a very hot day in the sun. When the morning came, I thanked God for our safety on that night. We could not help but see this big black snake crawling down the side of the rice burn.

Since we did not know what direction the snake was going in we put the hedged roll on fire to burn down the hedged roll. That was our LP site that night, trying to kill the snake. The snake crawled into the LP area as the fire continued to burn the brushes down.

After we picked up our claymore mines and trip flares, we started our walk back to our field base camp parameter, only to be informed that we had to go on an eagle flight the next day to another part of the jungle. Rick and Lemon were short timers now; they had very little time left in country, so they remained in the rear to be sent to Cu-Chi later.

After Lemon had heard about what happened to Stucky and Andy, he shot himself in the foot with his M–16. He said that it was an accident, but others were saying he did not want to go out to the field anymore, so he shot his foot to remain in Cu-Chi as long as possible, which was four months.

Lemon remained in the rear after he injured himself for four months, at which time he joined up with our company and platoon for that four-day mission. Lemon then returned to Cu-Chi, due to the amount of time he had remaining in Vietnam, removing him from the field.

The eagle flight took us to very heavy brush tree, jungle-like place. We were dropped off by the choppers and started sweeping the area once we were all off the choppers. To sweep this area, we looked into holes, brushes, trees, and the village area. You guessed it, no Viet Cong, but orders were for us to remain in the area overnight.

You see, this is what I mean by being stupid. On a sweep recon you do not carry a larger amount of ammo with you to engage into any heavy battle; just enough ammo to keep Sir Charles off your back if he is a sniper, not a Battalion or unit.

Any other contact from Sir Charles you would need to call in the artillery and mortar unit. If it is raining too hard neither of these units would be able to help you, including the gun ships; they cannot fly, nor can a pilot see when it's raining.

Many rounds of ammo would be needed when you're a distance away from the support unit and under heavy attack by the VC. You need support. To carry any more than twenty magazines becomes very heavy after two miles of walking in the heat and water. If nothing else, I remember how to pray. It is a weapon all by itself; God protected us from the foolishness of men of honor.

We set up our LP patrol, but as evening approached, I saw for the first time in my life, a bamboo viper. Man! That snake was fast and nearly invisible. If it wasn't for this guy who left his M–16 on the dirt, we would have never spotted this snake.

That snake changed his colors so quickly we only saw it because it was three or four different colors at once, as it crawled across the butt of the M–16. Yes! The viper got away, and we did not want to deal with this snake, red ants, Sir Charles, and these new C-ration or K-ration (instant food, add water, like dog food) on the same day, so we left that area to set up our LP elsewhere.

Well, thank God, there wasn't any activity that night. The choppers arrived that next morning to bring us further into the jungle where we had to chop our way through the heavy vines in this part of the jungle.

In the next few days we flew to a different area up north. It was hot, thick bushes and many craters in the ground that could have only been done by a jet bomber and bombs. It was identified by the size of the hole after the explosion.

The thick vines were very hard to move through in the jungle; the point man used a machete to cut the vines, while cautioned that he would not hit a trip wire to a booby trap.

Because of the thick vines, many of us switched with the point man to do some of the cutting as we walked point, allowing each man some rest from the cutting of the vine.

We moved through the area, ending up on the other side as we swept through the tall grass. We noticed the water at a distance; it was a canal. Maybe the VC used it to transport their supplies up and down the canal.

This location of the canal was radiod into our CP. The Captain informed us to set up an LP for the night to watch for VC activity, if they were transporting supplies to their troops up north or down south.

Once we made it through the other side we were exhausted and hungry. We wanted to turn around and go back. I could not help but to think about the 150 days I had left in country before I went home.

Many of the men that arrived in our company when Ed and I did, had been seriously wounded. Some died, and those that remained were on this mission. I started feeling like an old-timer and a short-timer, at the same time. That was a wonderful feeling.

I guess I've come a long way from many tears, fears, nervousness, anger, to plain bitterness and anger. No more tears; your buddies are dead, no time to cry or mourn, you had to keep on fighting or you'll be laying next to your dead buddy.

Who did you mourn for? Yourself, because inside of you was just as dead as your buddy that went home in that black body bag. Did you cry, do you have water to drink or water to wash your dirty face? Because tears could not be wasted on a dream, when no one was really killed.

Where are the tears, Wolfhound? Don't you just want to cry? Now is the time to release that pain that you buried so deep inside. After the first two bloody battles, you had died. The nice homeboy is a hired U.S. gunman.

But if I cry, I won't hear Sir Charles and this war has kept my eyes dry, for my return home. Was it too late, was I over the hill, who have I become? In just seven months, who have I become!

I was tired from no sleep, not enough food to eat, no

clean clothes. I don't know when I'd laughed with a lady. We often thought of home, because of the broken hearts and making up that made life what it really is. Happy times!

These seven months felt like seven years; there had been little distance between life and death. You cannot die unless you have lived or worse, died, because now you must be taught how to live. How young we were, when we came, and now, how old and tired we will be, if we leave. But as always, we must keep going forward, into what?

We patrolled the village area that day, with our new Lieutenant, the brother. We had checked out a night LP site and a rest site, before moving to the LP site later on that night.

By now I had been walking point for three months, and was walking point on this day, when we returned to our resting site. I noticed, as I stepped over the rice burn, that I had stepped over a trip wire and told everyone that I had done so.

The Lieutenant stopped the platoon and then told everyone to get down and to get ready to engage, with the VC if necessary. The Lieutenant told me to look around the parameter to see if I spotted any more trip wires. The wind started to blow very hard and strongly, then I noticed the movement of other trip wires, because of the blowing wind.

I told the Lieutenant that, because this parameter was booby trapped, I bet the LP site was also booby trapped. The Lieutenant had us moved out, heading towards the LP site. I was thinking, early on our sweep of these areas the rest location did not have booby traps in it earlier, and nor did the LP site that we had selected for tonight's ambush.

We finally reached the LP site. We walked in slowly, spreading out as each man entered this location. The wind started blowing really hard again, which set off a booby trap, where some guys were injured from the scrapped metal.

Jim went into the LP location. Many other guys had passed this booby trap. Jim stepped on the booby trap. It blew half of his foot off. The medic gave Jim some morphine to ease his pain. The medic then went to attend the other wounded guys.

I walked into the parameter. In front of me a little off to the right was a trip wire running from the tree branch to the ground. It was a booby trap.

Then a kid-Carson (a VC that is now willing to work with the American army after being captured) soldier walked in the location. I didn't say anything to him about the booby trap in another area, because I felt that he could still be a VC and may want to start shooting us. Then another guy stepped on a booby trap in another area.

The kid-Carson looked at me, then the VC opened gunfire on our location, with small weapon fire. After that, the kid-Carson stepped on that booby trap with the trip wire coming from the tree.

He cried for the medic, as did the others that were injured. I then went back to see Jim. Joe G., called me and said, that Jim was asking for me. "Two-Four." I need him, he said. I left my position and went to see what Jim wanted. Jim was in tears, asking himself if he was all right. He said, My foot is numb Two-Four. I told him not to look down. He said, Two-Four tell me the truth, did I lose my foot? I said, Part of it, but you'll be okay. Just hold on!

I told Joe G. to stay with Jim and guard the rear in case the VC move around to attack us from that direction. I went back to my spot and started firing my M–16 out front where the rounds from the VC were coming from.

I heard another crying out. It was the American-

Indian. The wind blew another trip wire that set off the booby trap, and he was hit. The point man was dead after he stepped on another booby trap that exploded.

The Lieutenant went to the other side. Boom! Boom!, another cry was heard agai. The Lieutenant had stepped on a booby trap. The gun battle between the local VC and us continued on even with the number of wounded soldiers from the booby traps.

The medic had his hands full and the VC was able to see our men falling from their booby traps, so they began laying down heavier fire power into our parameter. We had seven men down; then the medic stepped on a booby trap, trying to get to the other injured men. I then saw my short time getting shorter, by being overrun by the local VC, which had never entered my mind before.

Yates came over on the other side of me. I told him to place an M–79 HE (high-explosive) round about 150 meters to the left. He quickly popped two M–79 HE rounds in that location, as the remaining guys fired their M–16s. The VC then fled from the area. We now had to medic-vac eight guys out of the parameter.

We had radioed our company CP, LP patrol to tell them about our losses. They told us that they heard the gun battle, and the company was located about a mile away to the right of our LP parameter.

The choppers arrived to take the wounded and dead. It took almost two hours for the choppers to arrive, because of the gun fight with the VC. The choppers would not land in a hot LZ if they do not need to, they become an easy target. Later we told the pilots that the VC had left the area. Then the choppers landed and transported the injured and dead away to Cu-Chi hospital.

Then they left the rest of us. Ten men had to walk the mile to the company LP site. It was pitch dark out, so we gave our grid cores to the artillery unit, in order for them to shoot aerial flares that would light our way.

The illumination made us sitting ducks, but that was the only way we were able to move very quickly out of the area. We needed to be seen by our company, so they would not mistake us for the enemy.

The Sergeant was in charge now, so we put a ten-foot space between each man. We walked as the aerial flares illuminated the sky. When the flares would go down we would stop, get down, and take a count. Everyone knew there was just ten men, praying that the VC would not join our ranks on the end or ambush us.

The sky looked like day from the light of the flares. It really didn't matter if Sir Charles saw me because I was getting short from the stress of this night and not because of the time, I had left in country. It appeared that, as you got shorter, your chances for making it home grew less likely.

I prayed anyway; it helped me to cope with the darkness and the light from the flares, and the wounded and dead; and my own feeling of walking this night and the suffering I never knew until I arrived in Vietnam.

My peace is with God, for my life has flashed before me every minute that I remained in this country. For all the Caucasians that hated African-Americans, I would not wish this as punishment for them or anyone that was considered to be my worst enemy.

My father, step-mother, siblings and I attended church. We learned about Jesus Christ, who is love. Not fighting or killing and living in bad conditions such as these. Yes, it was hard for my father to provide for eight children, a wife, and himself, but God made a way out of no way. Do you understand that no one goes, before their time?

Many of us are punished so we return to God. In time

He will come. For life appeared to have been something of a wish, not something granted to you.

When we finally arrived at the company LP location, we received a welcome from the company as though we had not seen each other in years. It was just that bad here; that joy is one day, one moment at a time. The Captain shook each man's hand as others embraced us. Most of us shed a tear or two and we all welcomed this celebration of our arrival.

The ten of us were glad to have been out of that area, feeling that the VC would have returned with additional men and weapons to finish off the troops that remained. Our thinking was on target about 1:00 A.M. We saw the launching of the RPG rockets and heard AK-47 small weapon fire and other explosions in the area we had just left. They had also set off other booby traps from the scrapped metal of the RPG rockets as they continued their attack on that location. The VC ambush attack went on for about seven minutes, then they stopped. I guessed they realized that we had left the area, or that they had killed everyone, because they did not receive any return gunfire from that location.

The company had readied itself for the VC moving in this direction. We had taken a position in the parameter of our company, to pull guard duty for the rest of that night with the rest of the company.

It was a beautiful sight to see morning, as it has always been for me; that meant I had made another night and God wants me to do some good for others. The company saddled up and we moved in the direction of our field base camp, sweeping the area on the way back to the field base camp.

Breakfast was ready, nice and hot. I felt like I had not eaten in two weeks. The past two weeks we spent in the jungles, C-ration and K-rations are all we had had to eat, so I had not eaten for two weeks.

We had eggs, bacon, homefries, toast, orange juice, milk and seconds if we wanted. But I had enough from my first serving. After we ate, rest was the next step. The company pulled guard duty on the field base camp bunker line that night.

The next day we just stayed in the parameter and rested some more, because we had the night patrol to do. That night we received a report of heavy VC activity in the area. Our platoon was supposed to set up a LP patrol that night about one mile from the base camp parameter.

It was still very dark outside and we had only ten men left, so we told the sergeant that we would take sleeping quarters in the parameter and arrange with the front gate to say that we had left on the LP patrol.

This was that same sergeant that had wanted to send me on the LP patrol the last time we were on the Cambodian border. He now did not want to go out with just ten men when it was reported that there was heavy VC activity. So I took one of the radios and the sergeant had the other radio. As we squelched our radio back and forth to the CP, he helped us with this plan. (They monitor the squelch from the sergeant's radio and mine.) It was dark; you could not see your hands in front of you when you held them up.

This camp was five miles outside of Cu-Chi. When morning arrived, we gathered up all ten men and went outside of the gate and waited until 7:30 A.M. to enter, making it appear that we had been on the LP patrol all night.

The same night, about 2000 meters from the LP location, we would have set up the VC to attack an American line company. It was a heated battle, but questions were not asked of us. If the VC had come our way from them running from the battle, we did not have the fire power to hold them off if we were out there anyhow.

We continued doing our recons and sweeps of this area, as we looked for the VC, Sir Charles, The Viet Cong, The Gook, The Enemy, who liked to be a sniper, as he shoots his weapon at us and runs off, so he is not caught, while we swept through the area. We had an eagle flight back to the Providence area because they were still receiving rocket fire into the base camp.

We moved into this area to have our C-ration until it was night. We then would move to another location later that night. Ed, Joe G., and I were guarding a spot during the daylight hours, and as it became closer to nine o'clock our squad leader did not notify us that the company was moved back to a location before we were heading to our LP sight for the night.

The three of us were still talking softly when Sir Charles appeared five feet from where we were sitting. I saw Sir Charles first, but I was not sure if we had sent any of our men on the other side, if that was the reason for these men to be standing there in the first place.

At the same time Sir Charles saw us. I asked Joe G. and Ed, if they were part of our squad up in front and to our left, they said no. I said, Sir Charles is behind us, on three get the machine gun Ed. Then it happened; one, two, three. Ta-Ta-Ta-Ta-Ta-Ta-Ta-Ta-Ta-Ta-Ta. The VC was caught off guard, as much as we were. Ed slid behind his M–60 machine gun. Joe G. jumped over Ed to feed the ammo to the machine gun as Ed shot and hit several of the VC.

I had jumped at the same time that Ed and Joe G. did. I started firing my M–16 as Ed and Joe G. were firing the M–60 and provided cover for them. The VC I guess did not have any weapons other than the rockets they were carrying because they never fired a round as we moved out of that area.

We were running and were called by some of the men in our company from a location they were in. Everyone else was already there. No one told us that the rest of the platoon had moved back about 100 feet before going to our LP area for the night.

We were just left there by the Sergeant of our squad. I jumped on him verbally. The Captain and the Lieutenant kept me back and off the squad leader. Then the Captain selected a different site for the LP location. We moved into it. Later, after the Captain informed the CP that we were changing the LP site, because of the unexpected ambush, Ed, Joe G,. and I pulled on the VC.

This other site that was selected, had us running and dodging artillery rounds fired by our guys in the camp parameter. The artillery unit normally prep this location, at this time of night for Sir Charles, which had been used to launch VC rockets into the camp parameter and Providence in the past.

They fired four artillery rounds, but the last round I thought was indeed the last for everything. We covered our heads; we had no place to hide. That round hit and we heard someone crying out then we were all hit in our backs by the scrapped metal, or was it dirt?

I had said my prayers and was ready to walk into heaven. The sky was bright and then I raised my head. I said, I'm in heaven. Hey you guys, is everyone okay? It was this blond-haired guy. Then I knew I wasn't in heaven.

We were just hit very hard by rock fragments from the explosion, of the last artillery round. One man was injured and a chopper from Providence flew out to pick this guy up so he would have medical treatment. It was late by the time everyone was checked out to make sure no one else had been injured before the chopper left for Providence.

By the time we had set up the trip flares and claymore

mines in front of the area we were using for the LP site, it was late. It must have been about 2:00 A.M. when we saw rockets launched in the area that Ed, Joe G., and I had just ambushed the VC in. I guess the VC thought that that was our ambush sight when they were ambushing, so they launched their rockets thinking that we were still in that location.

The chopper arrived to medic-vac one wounded guy to the hospital. They wanted to get us, but thanks to God, He gave us wisdom to move elsewhere. The VC thought we were still in that area. The next morning we reconned the area where they had surprised Ed, Joe G., and I. We noticed a trail of blood and the bandages left by the VC from the ambush.

We followed the trail of blood back about 1000 meters. That led us to the location where the rockets had been launched from, but we did not find any VCs in the area. After reconning and sweeping the area for about two hours, we turned out sweep and moved into the direction of our camp parameter.

We returned to the field base camp later that morning. We reconned the area on our way back in. I relocated my package after all these months. It was sent from home, from my family. All the guys enjoyed the music and when they listened to the music they thought of home, wishing they could dance a little with some young lady.

XV

So Long to a Brother, a Friend in Nam

Ed Dow, from Texas, was leaving Vietnam, before I left for R&R (relaxation and recuperation). Ed's brother came to Nam as part of a communication group. He would not be exposed to any battle unless the VC overran Cu-Chi; then he would need to fight for his life.

Even though Cu-Chi was tunneled under in February 1969, the VC had thrown the saco charges at some of the helicopters, and blew five of them up. There was minor damage done to three others. Two men were killed and several were wounded but none of the VC escaped. There were nine of them; seven were killed, the other two captured and interrogated.

Cu-Chi had set up new bunker guard stations and destroyed the tunnels, placing steel piping underground to guard against future tunneling from the VC. The tree line on that side of the parameter was also moved back about 150 meters further than it was previously. They wanted to make Cu-Chi safe. Generals, Colonels, and Majors lived in Cu-Chi.

Ed's brother stood a better chance of surviving than Ed. His brother came to get Ed out of Vietnam. Ed would go to Germany as a Sergeant to complete his remaining time left in the service, or just for his time left in Vietnam. I was not sure how long he would be in Germany.

When Ed got on the convoy to Cu-Chi, I went in with him. It was hard for Ed and me to part company; we had been through so much and knew so much about one another. We were indeed brothers by friendship.

We cried as we had the first time we went on the convoy that took us to the field. This time it was for having the opportunity of knowing and having the love of a guy as a friend. I then met Ed's brother and greeted him with the Brother hand shake.

We talked and later that evening, went to the Wolfhound club. I bought Ed whatever he wanted and Ed bought me whatever I wanted. I only drank soda and Ed just wanted a couple of shots of whiskey; that was it.

The next day Ed and I departed. I felt that I would never see him again and he felt the same way. It was more likely that I might not return home alive than Ed because he was on his way to Germany.

We embraced each other and gave up the Brother hand shake, telling each other to pray for one another. I walked over to the convoy to return to the field base camp outside of the Cu-Chi area.

My R&R was scheduled for the last week in June. After I returned to the field we had a night mission for the first time in a long while. A cold chill ran down my spine knowing that the machine gunner was no longer Ed; it was someone that might not be as serious about making it home as Ed.

The attitude could create serious problems if we were under attack. I told the sergeant that I should not go out that night, but he said, Two-Four I need you. He said, you think you're nervous? We have twenty guys and twelve are newbys. I need some old timers to help if the VC hits us tonight. I realized that I had 78 days left in country and I didn't want any new guys doing anything stupid that would cost me my life. I told the new guys that they are to do nothing until we tell them to move, nor make any noise on this patrol and please stay awake on guard duty. I understood the sergeant's situation, so I agreed to go on the LP patrol with my platoon.

That night was a tough one, and I was super glad when morning arrived. After we swept our way back to the field base camp later that morning, the company was going into Cu-Chi, then to be re-located at a new camp on the other side of Tri-Nung.

The First Sergeant told me to remain out in the field until the next day. Then I would take the convoy into Cu-Chi to be processed for my R&R. Boy I was glad to hear that news. I saw many of the guys, including the Lieutenant Rogers (the Brother) that were wounded by the booby traps, on the LP site that night in May 1969.

The American-Indian re-enlisted for four more years to remain in Cu-Chi base camp. He talked about fighting until he was wounded. He extended his time in the service to stay out of the jungle.

Most of the guys were doing well. I told them that I was on my way to Thailand, Bangkok. They said, Enjoy yourself and come back to help us out in the field. I laughed and walked to the company barracks to sign in my weapon, ammo, and remaining gear and to sign out a class 'C' uniform, medals, shoes and other articles. I had left Joe G., Willie, and Doc Brown in the field, praying that all would be okay by the time I returned from my R&R.

I went to Thailand on my R&R, and I had a wonderful time there, taking pictures and seeing the temples. I met Nickie at the Soul Sister Club. I had a wonderful time with her. It was nice, not having on any boots or a weapon, and smelling badly all the time.

Even though it was a short time, I had not laughed with a lady and had so much joy in a while, like I had when I was in the States. I wanted this type of fun to last forever, but it was soon over, I told Nickie, thank you and good-bye. I had to leave Bangkok to return to Vietnam, to go out to the field again.

Once I returned I heard some real sad news. One of the new guys that had just arrived was killed, while I was away. He had picked up a box of grenades and started walking across the camp parameter. It exploded when he was in the center of the camp parameter.

Willie, Doc Brown, and many of the other guys were wounded and a few guys including the guy carrying the box of grenades were killed. Willie was hit by many pieces of scrapped metal and would be sent to the United States. He would receive a medical discharge from the service (million dollar wound), as others had received when they were seriously injured.

Doc left the field. He had put in seven months and was reassigned to the Cu-Chi medical area for the rest of his Vietnam tour. Now, Joe G. and I (Two-Four) were left out of the five brothers. But the company had returned to the prior field base camp, before I had arrived from my R&R, because they said that the parameter was too small for our company sizes.

Once I had arrived, the First Sergeant Major asked me if I wanted to go up to Nui-Bow-Den, (The Black Virginia Mountain) because of the time I had left in country (and also, because of what happened to Stucky and Andy, getting killed with less then 60 days left in- country).

I said let me think about it. Okay Serg, I'll let you know in the morning. The African-American Lieutenant and a few of the other guys that were wounded had returned to the field a few days earlier, before I returned from my R&R.

That night the Lieutenant wanted me to walk point, so I told him that I was a short-timer and would prefer just walking in the ranks. He agreed and we went off on LP patrol. It was still daylight when we left the parameter. I had thought of being in Thailand as I walked along the rice burn. It gave in when I stepped on it. I was daydreaming, back in Thailand.

I fell into the rice field filled with water. I just sat there wondering why I was still out in the field. Joe G. said, Two-Four you better wake up; you're no longer in Thailand, you're back in Nam, get with it, He then cursed___at me. As I looked at the water and mud while I sat there, they started pulling me up. I cleaned my M–16 as we continued our sweep to our LP site for that night.

I was glad I waited until I had ten months completed in-country, before I went on my R&R, otherwise it really would have been even more difficult for me, if I had six months left in Vietnam and had just returned from my R&R.

I then understood Rick's problem when Ed and I first arrived at the field after he had seen his wife, after six months in Nam. Nickie was not my wife, but just to be around women again almost made you forget about a war. It was finally dark, so we moved in the direction of our LP site for that night to ambush Sir Charles, if he passed our location.

It was so dark that night, we held on to the man's shirt in front of us as we walked. The darkness made it difficult to be sure Sir Charles did not join in the ranks of our platoon. Then we heard voices approaching, so we stopped and moved into the tree line. The sound grew closer and louder so we kneeled down and remained quiet.

Then the VC stopped right in front of us. The Lieutenant had passed the word not to open fire on them unless they moved in or started firing upon us. We were not sure how many VC were moving along the trail, but there were twenty of us. We were unable to count the number of VC due to the darkness, so we remained quiet until they had passed through the area.

I then felt something crawling on my hand. Ants, red ants. I had sat down on a nest of red ants. They were biting my hand, but I could not move or say anything. If I jumped, the VC would have heard the noise and might have opened fire on this area location.

We were told before our mission that one or two battalions of VC might be in this area location. Our platoon didn't have the opportunity to prepare ourselves to ambush the VC that night. The VC stopped talking as many other VC walked past. They had been talking; now they also decided to leave. Five minutes later we had not moved, yet we waited for 25 minutes more before we moved out.

Joe G. and another guy brushed the ants off my hands and back as quickly and quietly as they possibly could. We began moving out of the area one by one, each of us crossing this dim section, lit by heavy cloud coverage over the moon.

I stopped. I thought I had seen someone crossing at the same time that I was crossing. I was not sure if our platoon circulated around behind the VC. No, that was a VC. We started moving quickly away from this area.

After we had all crossed this section, we took a head count. Everyone was present, all twenty, or were the last few VC? The Lieutenant didn't like what he saw when he had crossed that section dimly lit by the moon. So he stopped again then walked down the line, asking each man their name. His M–16 was in the ready position. If you were a VC, he was going to blow you away.

Man it was bad. Then on top of that we set up our LP in a dried-out rice field and I was not aware of the water buffalo chips in this area. I lay on top of them. You could just imagine how I felt. I guess more than others, I was truly glad to see morning. We saddled up, took in the trip flares, and claymore mines, then reconned the area on our way back to the field base camp. As we moved into the village area, a water buffalo started running at us. I moved to the right, but this guy started shooting his M–16 in my direction. I then jumped down with the other guys that were in front of me, hitting the ground for cover.

This guy could not shoot at all. He almost killed us and missed the water buffalo. The water buffalo turned in another direction, heading for the hooch and the water buffalo pit, slowing down his speed. Then it stopped. The attack of the water buffalo forced the Lieutenant to move quickly to avoid the water buffalo horns. Everybody jumped on this crazy guy who was shooting his M–16 at us, with his crazy-looking self talking about the water buffalo was charging at him. I said, All you had to do was move to the right just like everyone else did. Shooting your weapon was not necessary.

I walked away and thought about what had happened since I returned from R&R. Two close encounters with the VC and then almost shot by one of our guys because of a water buffalo. When we arrived at our camp site, I didn't wait. I went over to the Sergeant Major (first Sergeant) and said, Good morning Sergeant Major. Remember what you asked me yesterday, if I wanted to go to Nui-Bow-Den? He said Yes. Well, my answer is yes.

I asked the Sergeant Major, When will I leave? He said, Today to Cu-Chi, then the other transportation arrangements will be made in a few days, okay? I said, Okay Sarg, and thank you. He said, Don't thank me; you deserve it. You're a good man Smith, I mean Two-Four. Then he and I just smiled at each other as I slowly started walking towards our bunker.

I had to tell Joe G. that I was going to the mountain, knowing that I did not want to leave him in the field by himself, because now four out of the five Brothers were no longer in the field with him. Joe G. said, I'm going to miss you Two-Four. I said, But I see now that I can no longer do this stuff in the jungle. Ever since I went on R&R, I miss home more now than ever.

Joe G. and I cried. We were friends, but Ed and I had a blood friendship. I loved Joe G. He was a funny guy. He also sang at his church, but he wanted to be known as the ladies' man, which I felt kept him from getting close to Ed, Will, Doc, and myself.

Joe G. would not let anyone say one bad word about me. Part of that was because I always read my military Bible every chance I got. He felt no one had a right to say anything about someone that felt that close to God. After we hugged and then gave up the Brother hand shake and the power sign, I was off to Cu-Chi on the convoy that afternoon.

I prayed that Joe G. would be okay in the field until he was sent on his R&R, which was scheduled for October 1969. He had arrived in Vietnam in December 1968. His tour of duty was up after his twelve months.

I took my tape recorder, ammo, M–16, canteens, gas mask, and some other goods that I had received in the package from home. I was then alone for the first time in Vietnam for two days. I had three meals a day and spent some time at the PX. It was either to do that, or do nothing. But I did not want to return to the field to see any action either.

Ten months, or was it ten years? I felt so different about everything. I never really dated until after the service and then, mentally, I was too old for many of the young ladies that were mentally less than 40 years of age.

After the two days in Cu-Chi, I was transported to Nui-Bow-Den by a shounook helicopter. It took 45 minutes for the helicopter to reach the top of this mountain. That day was sunny and it was hot in the month of July 1969, but I would be able to relax a little until I went home.

Nui-Bow-Den had been overrun twice since I had been in Vietnam. Many men were killed during those attacks by the Viet Cong. That was the reason I didn't tell the Sergeant Major yes right away.

I prayed to God about this move to the mountain and I felt it was answered that night, when I was out on the LP patrol with my platoon. I could not afford to stop praying, no matter what the cost might be. It has strengthened me in more ways than I can tell you.

Once I arrived on Nui-Bow-Den, the Major, First Sergeant, Captain, and a few other guys greeted me on the helicopter pad. Then they informed me of the rules and regulations they had on the mountain.

The Captain had the guy from the bunker they had assigned me to meet me, then he took me to the bunker. I guess these officers felt a need to tell me about drugs (pot). They just didn't understand anything about the jungle, with their spit shine boots and starched fatigues.

XVI

The Trip Home after the Duty on the Mountain

The percentage of guys that smoked pot may have been less than one percent; maybe or two guys out of two hundred guys, No drugs played a part in my life. We had supper in the mess hall. It was hot and tasted really good. I met some of the other guys as they entered the mess hall. Many of these guys wanted to know if I had seen any action, and if so, how was it?

I did not want to go into any details about my field experience with the VC so I just told the guys that I could not talk about it at this time. So they said that they understood, and said that they would see me later in the mess hall.

That night I didn't know what was going on at the bottom of the mountain. About a thousand meters from the base of the mountain there were red tracers flying back and forth from one side to the other.

I asked this guy at the bunker named Paul what type of fire works celebration was going on. He said, that's no celebration, that's a fire fight between the Viet Cong and the American soldiers. It looks like the VC are winning. He laughed, then walked away.

I continued watching the battle and then started praying for the American unit and the VC to stop this killing. It was about 10:00 P.M. By 10:30 P.M., the battle had stopped; it was over.

This guy Paul on this bunker line had never been in the field, but had been blessed to be on the mountain since his arrival in Nam. He had no respect for the battle he viewed from the top of this mountain. To him it was a war movie.

Even though I was many hundreds of feet above this battle, which appeared to be on television, my heart, mind, and body was at the bottom of the mountain in the middle of this fire fight. I understood the battle and what the American soldiers were thinking.

That night I pulled guard duty. Every two hours was the schedule we shared as part of our responsibility to guard the parameter. The guy Paul at my bunker shared with me that the three bunkers to our left were overrun by the VC six months ago, prior to his arrival.

He also said that since then they have installed new barbed wire, three roll wide and three rolls high around the parameter. He was also told that tigers, lions, and snakes had been a problem, after the Americans took this mountain from the VC.

He told me that a tiger pulled a soldier out of a fox hole. They did not kill the tiger, but they did wound it and the soldier had to be medic-vacced to the hospital. He had to receive several stitches in his arm and shoulder, from the bites and claws of the tiger.

It had been a long time since I slept in a bed, outside of being on R&R. That night I went to my bunk and just laid there, thinking about Ed in Germany, Joe G. in the field, Willie who went back to the United States because of his injuries, Doc Brown who was back in Cu-Chi, and some of the guys who died: Peewee, Hudson, Stucky, Andy, Sergeant Williams, Sergeant Peter, Charles, Meatball, Paul, Ray, the other two Captains and four Lieutenants, CP RTOs, many new guys that did not have a chance to understand this war, and all the other guys that didn't make it this far. To their family and friends, God Bless you.

The guys that came and were able to get out of the field like Yates, Rick, Lemon, Robert Brown, Doc Brown, Sergeant Major from the Philippines, Lieutenant Nebask, Captain Coronet, Lieutenant Johnson, Miller, Red, Sergeant George, The American-Indian, the Indian, Jim, and many others. I just don't remember all the names. God Bless you and your memories. Memories, I pray that you are able to live with them.

I thought about Madlock. What was he doing in Charlie company? Was he still alive? All the rest of the Wolfhounds, they had dared Sir Charles to walk over them if he was able.

Tears formed in my eyes and flowed through my heart. I knew then I was hurt somewhat by the terror of life; a puzzle with many missing pieces that might never be put together to form that beautiful picture I needed to go forward.

We were 19 years old when we left home, and the ones that would return home might or might not be mentally all right. It may have been one year away from home, according to the calendar, but it was far longer mentally. We boys, the ones that would make it back, would never have the truth told to us about the why and what for of the war. We loved each other and we did what we could for each other. The lie that one wanted to tell, would quickly be stopped; he would look and the truth came forth.

The two hours of the other guy's guard was up. He came down and said, Oh gee, I thought you were asleep. You're on guard duty, now. I got off my bunk as he was undressing to get into his bunk and I shook my head (indicating that he just didn't know and he could care less). I walked out the door of the bunker, two steps up that led me to the guard station on top of our bunker.

The artillery units were shooting up aerial flares every 15 to 20 minutes to illuminate the area, helping us to see any VC movement towards the parameter. We also had a starlight-scope that was used to detect any movement of Sir Charles during the night. On my guard watch I took my M 16 to the guard station. As the aerial flares illuminated the sky I saw a shadow.

I didn't know if it was a friend or Sir Charles. I switched my weapon from safety to semi-automatic. Then the door to the guard station opened quickly. I removed the slack out of the trigger to fire. The Major had opened the door. I had quickly heard his voice. Smith, he said. I eased up on the trigger as he walked in the door. Smith, I just wanted to inform you that headquarters said that they received information that the VC were moving up the mountain to over take this command post.

I said, Okay, I'll keep watch for the VC; but I also said, Major, the next time call out first, before you open the door, because I was going to kill you except that you called my name as you entered the door. The Major said that he had called my name, but I didn't answer him earlier. He continued, I will call your name louder the next time, because I know that you will shoot me if I don't.

Then the Major said, please tell the next guy that will pull guard duty this information. I said that I would, as the Major left the guard station. I had to remain on the mountain for two months, before I was able to return home. It was different on the mountain this time. I used the time to find out something in my life and the effects of Vietnam.

The next morning I went to the medical officer bunker to have my ears examined, because the Major had stated that he called me earlier and I did not want my hearing to be a problem for me after the previous night's incident.

The doctor said that I had an infection in both ears and a hole in my left eardrum and that it was possible that a hole could be in the right ear too. He gave me some medicine to clear up the infection and alleviate the pain. He advised me to check with the VA hospital regarding my ear problem once I returned to the States, because he did not have the medical equipment to do so in his office on the mountain.

Several days later, I received mail from a friend named Ronnie. He was in the 1st Calvary Unit. He drove a fuel truck, re-fueling the choppers in the Providence (Tan-Nang) area. I wrote him back and told him that I was now stationed on the Black Virgin mountain. I gave him a phone number to call me when he got a chance between the re-fueling of the choppers.

About a month later, Ronnie called me. It was August. The radio operator came to my bunker to get me. He said, you have a phone call. I said to myself, Who could be calling me, spending that kind of money to make this long distance call to Vietnam. At the same time I thought it was my parents calling me. All that I could think about was, How did they find out where I have been stationed.

Then I picked up the phone and said, Hello. Ronnie said, Joe, it's me Ronnie. It's been very hard to reach you; I tried to call you, but I always lost the call before the operator down here could make a connection. Even then it was very difficult talking and listening, because the signal grew weaker every second.

I knew Ronnie had made the call, but I wanted to say something, when I had my chance. I said, Ronnie can you hear me? I'm fine. The signal grew weaker. He said, Joe I'm losing you I'll talk to you again okay?

Then the signal just broke off and the static took over the air waves. But it was nice just hearing his voice again, even if it was just for a few seconds. We knew that the both of us, were still alive and that's what really counted.

The routine was the same every day, just like the routine in the field, and the routine we followed back in the States. It was just a different routine, but a routine nevertheless. With a month left in Nam, I was enjoying the three meals each day. I liked it, along with the clean clothes, shower, and having a bunk bed to sleep in each night, and not having to lay on the ground like I did in the fields. Plus, I no longer had to do any more patrols.

Can you dig this? I was short. Tears started to form in my eyes as I thought about Joe G. still in the fields, when the rest of the group had been sent, elsewhere. Ed was in Germany, Doc Brown was in Cu-Chi, Willie was back in the States, Miller was in Cu-Chi, and me, I was on the mountain top.

That day we received information that Sir Charles was on Nui-Bow-Det, a smaller mountain to the left of Nui-Bow-Den. The movement of the VC would place them to the middle of Nui-Bow-Den once they crossed over from Nui-Bow-Det.

The bombers wanted to drop some napalm on Nui-Bow-Det and in the middle of Nui-Bow-Den, but I guess the commander on the mountain, must have given them the go-ahead because the bombers dropped the napalm. You heard the explosion and saw the flames after the planes turned the nose of their plane upward as it made its pass.

They wanted the guys on the bunker lines to be ready for action, if Sir Charles ran to the top of the mountain during or after the air strike. The red alert was on. No one could rest until this was over. Then the clouds rolled in that made it nearly impossible to see anything or anyone five feet in front of you. That meant that if we were under attack no one would be able to help us until the clouds were burned away by the sun or the winds blew the clouds away. Man, this was bad; I'm short, I have very little time left, I said. No I would not get killed being in the fields, but could be killed on the mountain.

The aerial flares helped just a little in some cases, and made it worse in other cases. It was difficult to see in front, on the side, and in back of you. This was a long three days and nights living in the clouds, with a red alert, because the VC were on the move to the mountain top, because this was a good time for them to attack.

That morning, after no sleep for the three days, I saw the sun peek through the clouds. That was a beautiful morning sight to see. The guy at my bunker said he had to get some sleep each night or he would not be able to function at all. Sleeping or the lack of sleep was something that was normal for me. After being up for three days without rest I just went back to my normal behavior to survive. Thank God for the outcome.

I sat up or laid down, but felt like I had to be ready for action, just like when I was on the Cambodian border. We then received some more information from headquarters: 1st Calvary had captured some of the VC during an ambush patrol that was set up at the base of the mountain.

Many of the VC were killed during this ambush and from the bombers' air strike. They captured about twenty or more VCs. The duty on the mountain went back to the normal guard duty on the bunkers once this event was over with the VCs.

Five days before I left the mountain to be processed out of Vietnam, there was tear gas dropped on Nui-Bow-Den. Many of the guys did not have a gas mask, so they just coughed. I had mine from the field. I cleared it, then placed it over my head and started breathing.

Gas had been dropped from 'you guessed it' our planes, but the wind shifted and blew the gas upward. It happened so quick that everyone was running for cover. Before this event, my gas mask had not been used; now the order of the men was disrupted, because of the gas.

The time finally arrived. I had to go home. My bags were packed, the little that I had, and I had my tape player in my hands, ready to go. The Caucasian guy at my bunker looked at me. I shook his hand then he hugged me. He was shaking like a leaf on a tree on a windy day.

He said, I'm going to miss you. Take care, I'll remember what you told me, Two-Four, everything! As I looked from the bunker I could see the chopper coming up, clearing the mountain top, coming in for a landing.

I went back inside the bunker to get my things. Then I heard, Two-Four! Two-Four! I said, that sounds like Joe G., but it couldn't be. I ran out of the bunker. There he was, running for his life, in my direction. I ran to meet him. We jumped into each other's arms and hugged each other. We both tried to talk.

The Major said, Smith, come on, the chopper is leaving. I said this is one of the guys from my company; he's a Wolfhound. The Major then told the pilot to give me a few more minutes.

We cried again, Joe G. and I. He was coming to and I was leaving the mountain. I gave him my tapes and tape player to have some music to listen to, as it reminded him of home. I told him good-bye and again gave up the Brother hand shake. Then I left to board the chopper.

Just those few minutes that we spent together were so good. He'll remain on the mountain until December 1969. It was September 1969 now. Joe G. was no longer in the fields, thank God.

After our 45-minute flight from the mountain, I went

to the orderly room to start the processing of my paper work. At first I thought they were going to send me to Cu-Chi for processing because I was in Providence, but they did everything right there. As I sat there, I envisioned myself kissing the U.S. soil once I returned home.

I had about two hundred dollars of M.P.C. (Military Payment Currency) in my pocket, so I stood in line like everyone else to exchange my money for the U.S. green-backs. This guy, a brother, asked me to exchange some of his money when I went to the exchange window. I guess he had about a thousand dollars or more from gambling, so I exchanged it for him and waited until he was able to come through the line. You were only able to exchange four hundred dollars of M.P.C. money per person.

Then a couple of brothers asked me, after we had exchanged our money, if I wanted to check out some boom-boom girls before we went home. I told them, No, I'm going home to take care of that; I'm not going to have anything happen to me now!

The next morning we got on the truck to Cu-Chi. Once we had arrived, I saw this Caucasian guy that I was in basic training with. We were glad to see each other. He told me about some of the other guys that I knew that did not make it. Then someone walked up behind me and hit me. I turned around; it was Charles Madlock. Boy, we hugged and talked, and hugged and talked.

I introduced Ray to Charles. Ray and I hugged. I told him that I will see him in Connecticut. We shook hands; then he left. I then told Charles that Ed was sent to Germany, and that he was able to go there because his brother came to Nam to get him out of the field.

Madlock said he almost went home in a body bag too many times. He had heard about Sir Charles overrunning our parameter on the border. He said, he could see Ed and me running now, keeping Sir Charles at a distance off our backs.

Madlock would have come to Ben-Hoa with me, but his orders directed him to depart from Cam-Ram-Bay, so we departed. That next night, we visited the officers' club. The Vietnamese women looked better in the officers' club and we got a message before we left Nam.

The date was Tuesday, September 12, 1969. The plane ride home was in silence. I just thanked God for everything. I looked out of the window of the plane. I felt that I had had a terrible dream. Because all that stuff, that I thought I saw, could not have been for real.

There was no way in life that I could have lived like that, through all kinds of stuff. I looked at myself. When I went to the rest room I looked in the mirror, I guess to see if I had become a beast from this terrible dream I had had.

I thought of many things as I took this trip home. Now that my fighting was over in Vietnam, I still had a fight to continue within the United States to receive my civil rights.

After the sixteen hours of flying, we landed in California at the Air Force Base airport where they had dogs and other soldiers. We were rushed off the plane. My feeling for kissing the ground left quickly. I did not want to kiss anything after I arrived in the U.S.

I had one red-checked suitcase and a duffelbag. The people at the airport looked at me as though I had done something wrong. The other soldiers walked around our luggage with these dogs, having the dogs smell the bags for dope, I guess.

Someone said, Do you have anything to claim. I was taken off guard by the type of welcome we received. No one showed us any loving or caring spirit. One, two, three, you were in and out. No one even cared about what you had been through.

This man, I guess he had asked me earlier if I had anything to claim, asked me again. I turned and looked at him; then he took my arm and bag and led me through this door to board the bus. He never checked my bags.

I guess when he saw my facial expression from all of the activity that was going on, he must have said, let me get this guy out of here, before he explodes and goes off on me and everyone else. But I was cool, just a little taken aback.

There were some Vietnamese people at our next location. Some Caucasian guy exploded when they saw these Vietnamese people. Four brothers and myself had to hold these six Caucasian guys back. They were cursing and wanted to hurt these Vietnamese people. One guy said. Look at them, they don't have a scratch on them and my friends are dead.

The African-American brothers told these Caucasians not to fight these Vietnamese people, because if they did, they would be put in jail and wouldn't be able to go home. They cooled down and listened this time. We all got dressed and then left for the airport. Once I arrived in Connecticut, my brother Warren met me. I called home from the airport in California to tell him the flight and the time that I would arrive.

Welcome home Joe, Warren said, I missed you. I'm glad you made it back alive. He hugged me and then picked me up. Joe, I'm glad you're home. We then got in his car and headed for home. Yes, I'm a Wolfhound forever!!